The Small Museum Toolkit, Book 6

About the Series

The American Association for State and Local History Book Series publishes technical and professional information for those who practice and support history, and addresses issues critical to the field of state and local history. To submit a proposal or manuscript to the series, please request proposal guidelines from AASLH headquarters: AASLH Book Series, 1717 Church St., Nashville, Tennessee 37203. Telephone: (615) 320-3203. Fax: (615) 327-9013. Website: www.aaslh.org.

About the Organization

The American Association for State and Local History (AASLH), a national history organization headquartered in Nashville, TN, provides leadership, service, and support for its members, who preserve and interpret state and local history in order to make the past more meaningful in American society. AASLH is a membership association representing history organizations and the professionals who work in them. AASLH members are leaders in preserving, researching, and interpreting traces of the American past to connect the people, thoughts, and events of yesterday with the creative memories and abiding concerns of people, communities, and our nation today. In addition to sponsorship of this book series, the Association publishes the periodical *History News*, a newsletter, technical leaflets and reports, and other materials; confers prizes and awards in recognition of outstanding achievement in the field; and supports a broad education program and other activities designed to help members work more effectively. To join the organization, go to www.aaslh.org or contact Membership Services, AASLH, 1717 Church St., Nashville, TN 37203.

The Small Museum Toolkit, Book 6

Stewardship: Collections and Historic Preservation

Edited by
Cinnamon Catlin-Legutko
and Stacy Klingler

AltaMira
PRESS

A division of
ROWMAN & LITTLEFIELD PUBLISHERS, INC.
Lanham • New York • Toronto • Plymouth, UK

Published by AltaMira Press
A division of Rowman & Littlefield Publishers, Inc.
A wholly owned subsidiary of The Rowman & Littlefield Publishing Group, Inc.
4501 Forbes Boulevard, Suite 200, Lanham, Maryland 20706
http://www.altamirapress.com

Estover Road, Plymouth PL6 7PY, United Kingdom

British Library Cataloguing in Publication Information Available

Library of Congress Cataloging-in-Publication Data

The small museum toolkit. Book 6, Stewardship : collections and historic preservation / edited by Cinnamon Catlin-Legutko and Stacy Klingler.
    p. cm. — (American Association for State and Local History book series)
  Includes bibliographical references and index.
  ISBN 978-0-7591-1953-6 (cloth : alk. paper) — ISBN 978-0-7591-1340-4 (pbk. : alk. paper) — ISBN 978-0-7591-1347-3 (electronic)
  1. Small museums—Collection management. 2. Museum conservation methods.
I. Catlin-Legutko, Cinnamon. II. Klingler, Stacy, 1976– III. Title: Stewardship : collections and historic preservation.
  AM141.S63 2012
  069'.5—dc23   2011028452

∞™ The paper used in this publication meets the minimum requirements of American National Standard for Information Sciences—Permanence of Paper for Printed Library Materials, ANSI/NISO Z39.48-1992.

Printed in the United States of America

CONTENTS

EDITORS' NOTE

Small museums are faced with the enormous task of matching the responsibilities of a large museum—planning strategically, securing and managing human and financial resources, providing stewardship of collections (including historic buildings) as well as excellent exhibitions, programs, and publications, and responding to changing community and visitor needs—all with more limited human and financial resources. Small museum staff (paid or unpaid) often fulfill key responsibilities outside their area of expertise or training.

We recognize that small museum staff lack time more than anything. To help you in the trenches, we offer this quick reference, written with your working environment in mind, to make the process of becoming a sustainable, valued institution less overwhelming.

The Small Museum Toolkit is designed as a single collection of short, readable books that provides the starting point for realizing key responsibilities in museum work. Each book stands alone, but as a collection they represent a single resource to jump-start the process of pursing best practices and meeting museum standards.

If you are new to working in museums, you may want to read the entire series to get the lay of the land—an overview of what issues you should be aware of and where you can find resources for more information. If you have some museum training but are now responsible for more elements of museum operations than in your previous position, you may start with just the books or chapters covering unfamiliar territory. (You might be wishing you had taken a class in fundraising right about now!) As you prepare to tackle new challenges, we hope that you will refer back to a chapter to orient yourself.

While any chapter can be helpful if read in isolation, we suggest that you start with the first book, *Leadership, Mission, and Governance*, and look at the issues of mission, planning, and assessment. You will find that almost every chapter asks you to consider its subject in light of your mission and make decisions based on it. As you begin to feel overwhelmed by all the possible opportunities and challenges you face, assessment and planning will help you focus your scarce resources strategically—where you need them the most and where they can produce the biggest impact on your organization. And this book offers tips for good governance—defining the role of a trustee and managing the director-trustee relationship. Understanding this relationship from the outset will prevent many headaches down the road.

Financial Resource Development and Management offers you direction about how to raise and manage money and stay within your legal boundaries as a nonprofit. How to manage resources, human and inanimate, effectively and efficiently is discussed in *Organizational Management. Reaching and Responding to the Audience* encourages you to examine your museum audiences and make them comfortable, program to their needs and interests, and spread the word about your good work.

The remaining two books explore the museum foundational concepts of interpretation and stewardship in a small museum setting. *Interpretation: Education, Programs, and Exhibits* considers researching and designing exhibits and best practices for sharing the stories with your audiences. *Stewardship: Collections and Historic Preservation* rounds out the six-book series with an in-depth look at collections care, management, and planning.

We would like to thank the staff at the American Association for State and Local History and AltaMira Press, our families, and our colleagues for encouraging us to pursue this project. You have tirelessly offered your support, and we are incredibly grateful.

There is little reward for writing in service to the museum field—and even less time to do it when you work in a small museum. The contributors to this series generously carved time out of their work and personal lives to share with you their perspectives and lessons learned from years of experience. While not all of them currently hang their hats in small museums, every one of them has worked with or for a small museum and values the incredible work small museums accomplish every day. We offer each and every one of them more appreciation than we can put into words.

We hope that this series makes your lives—as small museum directors, board members, and paid and unpaid staff members—just a little bit easier. We hope that we have gathered helpful perspectives and pointed you in the direction of useful resources.

And when you are faced with a minor annoyance, a major disaster, or just one too many surprises, remember why you do this important work and that you are not alone.

It takes a very special kind of person to endure and enjoy this profession for a lifetime. Not a day passes in which I do not learn something, or find something, or teach something, or preserve something, or help someone.

—Unknown author

Keep up the good work!

Cinnamon Catlin-Legutko
Stacy Lynn Klingler
Editors

PREFACE

I have a confession to make. Until I got to the American Association for State and Local History (AASLH), I never truly understood what it was to work in a small museum. Sure, I had been around them, visited them, talked to my peers who worked in them both as paid and unpaid (read: volunteer) staff, and appreciated the role they play in the historical narrative and in communities. But I never *got it* until I got to AASLH.

So what have I learned? First and foremost, small museums are the bedrock of the American museum profession. You will not find museums the size of the Smithsonian or historic sites like Gettysburg in every American community, but you will often find a small museum, sometimes more than one. While we in the historical profession talk often about how we are the keepers of the American past, and we are, those who work in the smaller institutions are truly minders of our nation's patrimony and heritage. They care for the objects and history of communities throughout the country, stories that would probably be lost without that care. Quite simply, without small museums, our knowledge of the past, our historical narrative, would be incomplete.

The second thing I have learned, and been truly humbled by, is the passion and dedication small museum professionals and volunteers have for their craft. You will rarely hear small museum professionals complaining about a lack of resources—that is just part and parcel of the task at hand. Instead of attacking a challenge with reasons for why something cannot be done, they redirect their thoughts to how it can be done within the parameters provided. So, small museum professionals are equally comfortable with answering the phone, giving a tour, processing collections, and plunging the occasional toilet (the latter falling into the "other duties as assigned" category in a job description).

And amid all that, small museum professionals keep a great sense of humor. At several gatherings of small museum folks over the years, we have had fun with a game we call "You Know You Work in a Small Museum If . . ."

Responses ranged from "A staff meeting consists of all staff members turning around in their office chairs at the same time" to "You're the director, but if you're the first one to work after a snowstorm, you get to shovel the sidewalk and plow the parking lot." But my absolute favorite was "When you walk through the gallery and hear a guest say, 'The staff should really do . . .' and you think, Hey, *I'm* my staff!"

At one time, as Steve Friesen of the Buffalo Bill Museum and Grave notes in chapter 2 of Book 1 of this series, the term *small museum* was used as a pejorative. Small museums were underfunded, under-resourced, and poorly managed. "If they weren't," the thinking went, "they'd be large museums, right?" Wrong. Being small does not mean you aspire to be big or that the institution is small because it is doing something wrong. Smallness has more to do with a spirit and dedication to a certain niche of history, a community, a person, a subject.

I believe the field has moved beyond that prejudice, and small museums are now celebrated. At AASLH we often discuss how much larger museums can learn from smaller institutions about how to serve as effective stewards of their resources and to engage their communities in a deep, meaningful way. There is much to learn from small museums, and our peers and colleagues at those institutions are ever willing to share.

Along this line, I have always found that one of the best things about the museum profession in general is how open it is with regard to sharing ideas and processes and just offering support. In no corner of the field is this more evident than in the world of small museums. Small museum professionals are founts of wisdom and expertise, and every small museum session, luncheon, or affinity event I have been to has been packed, and discussion has been stimulating and often inspiring. In fact, discussion often spills out into the hallways after the formal session has concluded.

But the work I know best is that of the AASLH Small Museums Committee. The editors of this series, Cinnamon Catlin-Legutko and Stacy Klingler, are, respectively, the founding and current chairs of this committee. Under their leadership, a team of small museum folks has completed a set of ambitious goals, including gathering a variety of research and developing a small museum needs assessment, presenting sessions at conferences throughout the country, and raising money for scholarships to send peers to the AASLH annual meeting each year. It is this last item I want to highlight as it gives the clearest example of the love and commitment those in small museums have for each other.

In my view, the fact that the Small Museums Committee successfully organizes an annual fundraising campaign is commendable. The fact that it routinely raises money to send *two* people to the meeting (and four people in some years) is truly remarkable. This is indicative of the passion and dedication small museum professionals feel toward the cause of small museums and toward their colleagues. Let's face it, history professionals are not at the top of the salary food chain. (I always note this whenever I speak to history classes about a career in public history. "If you choose this career, you are going to love what you do; you are going to be making a difference in your community. But you are also taking a vow of poverty. No one goes into the history field to get rich.") And while donors to this fund are not all from small museums, small museum professionals are a large part of the pool, giving as generously as anyone. I am so heartened each year as we raise this money.

So, what does all this have to do with the book in your hands? I would say a lot. First, the contributors are small museum professionals or aficionados themselves. They are dedicated to the craft in the small museum environment and know firsthand its needs and challenges. In addition, they have been involved with, and led national discussions on, these issues. They are passionate about the cause of small museums, and they have organized and written a book (and series) that offers a variety of voices and contexts while speaking to the needs as articulated. The thirty-plus contributors to this series offer a wealth of experience and expertise in dealing with the complex nature of running a small museum, in preserving traces of the American past for future generations, often on a shoestring budget and with limited resources. It is a lesson we can all learn. And it is a lesson well articulated here.

Whether you are a seasoned small museum professional, a newly minted executive director, or a museum studies or public history student, it is my hope that this book series will give you the tools you need to succeed in your job. I also hope that you will continue to carry the torch for small museums in your community and in the larger museum field. The field needs your passion and expertise, and the role you fill in your community is critical.

Bob Beatty
Vice President, AASLH

CHAPTER ONE
CARING FOR THE FUTURE: COLLECTIONS CARE BASICS
Scott Carrlee

Books have the same enemies as people: fire, humidity, animals, weather, and their own content.

—Paul Valery

This chapter on collections care basics is grounded in three principles:

1. Solutions for collections care issues must be grounded in the same reality in which museums operate with regard to resources (time, money, staffing, etc.).
2. Collections care is a continuum: Inside is better than outside; on a shelf is better than on the floor; in an enclosure is better than out in the open. A museum can always improve, no matter where it is on the continuum.
3. Preventive conservation is the most cost-effective way of caring for collections. Rarely is it considered glamorous. It employs common-sense strategies to protect collections.

Collections care is a heavy responsibility. Marie Malaro states in *A Legal Primer on Managing Museum Collections*, "A museum has a responsibility to provide reasonable care to the objects that are entrusted to it."[1] The field is left to determine what reasonable care means. She also notes that "if the matter at issue directly concerns collection policy (the core function of the museum) courts have been inclined to expect a higher standard."[2] The American Association of Museums (AAM) defines a standard as "a generally accepted level that all museums are expected to achieve."[3] The AAM standard for stewardship of collections reads, "The institution legally, ethically and effectively manages, documents, cares for and uses the collections."[4] Considering the complexity of some collections care issues, that is a remarkably simple sentence. Museum standards are general in order to apply to all types of museums. The meaning of effective care for each type of museum is determined by the different disciplines within the field. What works for transportation museums does not necessarily apply to art museums.

This chapter is organized into sections for each of the six general threats to collections:

1. Climate
2. Light
3. Pests
4. Pollutants
5. Human interaction
6. Disasters

This chapter aims to help you create a preservation environment: one that promotes collections care rather than allows preventable damage to occur. Creating a preservation environment for collections should be the goal of every museum. I hope to provide information that jump-starts that process and helps museums move up the collections care continuum. This chapter presents the basics, not an encyclopedia, of collections care. Rather than provide information on a given topic in an exhaustive manner, I summarize key information that I have gleaned over twenty years of working in museums. These are concepts and a few good ideas that I think everyone working in museums should know. I have tried to be practical and succinct without resorting to boilerplate answers for complex issues. The chapter is meant to be a starting point, not the final word. Once you have mastered this information, you are ready to continue to educate yourself with further readings and research.

1. Climate: At Home in the Range

Conservation is humanity caring for the future.

—Nancy Newhall

In Canyon de Chelly National Monument on the Navajo Nation in northern Arizona, I once had the privilege of visiting a dry cave site off-limits to tourists. Our guide, a National Park Service archaeologist, made sure we did not step on any of the artifacts left behind by those who occupied the site long before Europeans even thought of exploring this continent. One of those artifacts was the remnant of a woven sandal made of plant fibers that still held the shape of the owner's foot. It was right there, on the surface, some seven hundred years after it had been discarded. There had been no conservator or curator to care for it, no climate-controlled storage room to protect it, no sealed exhibit case to display it in. It was just lying there undisturbed for centuries in its own preservation environment.

Providing a stable climate is the key to preserving museum collections. This is often the first thing people talk about when referring to collections care. Yet climate is, without a doubt, the most difficult and expensive to manage of all the threats to collections. Recent studies indicate that the common museum wisdom of adhering to a single set point for climate control is not the best course of action for protecting collections (or for sustaining the Earth's environment, for that matter). It turns out that keeping the climate within a given range and not allowing it to go to extremes for extended periods is enough to provide an acceptable level of care for collections. This is good news for small museums. It means that we can put our efforts toward more realistic goals for climate control and still have resources left for mitigating other threats to collections.

What Is Climate?

In the context of museums, climate is the temperature and relative humidity (RH) of the space in which collections are stored or exhibited. Climate control refers to the ability to heat and cool a space and to add or remove moisture from the air. Most of the time this is achieved through a heating, ventilating, and air conditioning (HVAC) system. If you do not have an HVAC system in your building, chances are you do not have climate control. Frequently, small museums do not have climate control. Many small museums are in older or historic buildings where only heating is provided in the winter.

The absence of climate control does not mean that a preservation environment is impossible to achieve or that you can do nothing to improve your climate situation. The most important thing is to monitor your climate and use that information to make meaningful changes that improve collections care.

Why is humidity relative?

We often use the word "humidity" when talking about the effects on museum collections. What we mean is "relative humidity." In plain speaking, relative humidity refers to how much water vapor is in the air compared with how much water vapor could be in the air at a given temperature. The key here is that it depends on, or is relative to, the temperature.

How Does Climate Impact Collections?

Climate affects collections in three ways: chemically, biologically, and mechanically.[5] Temperature and RH are two major factors in controlling the rate at which chemical reactions occur and therefore how fast artifacts deteriorate. Basically, the higher the temperature, the faster an object decays. Mold, bacteria, and insects benefit from high RH. Water is life, so the more water there is (even in the air), the more these living entities will prosper and can potentially damage artifacts. Mechanical damage occurs when organic materials absorb and give off moisture over extended periods. The relative humidity of the museum environment governs the amount of moisture in artifacts. As RH moves into high and low extremes for extended periods, the artifacts experience the change and are damaged by it.

What Can You Do about Climate?

You often read on a box of dry goods, "Keep in a cool, dry place." The same is true for museum artifacts. Just think of that cave site where the sandal was preserved for centuries. It was in a cool, dry place. Yet, for museums, it is difficult to replicate the environment of a dry cave. The people who visit and work at museums have their own climate needs, which are often at odds

Photo 1.1. Splits in skin-covered kayak caused by unstable climate. (Photo by Scott Carrlee)

4

Table 1.1. Effects of Climate

Material	Cause	Effect
Wood	(low RH)	Splitting/cracking
Leather/skin	(low RH)	Cracks/tears
Baskets	(low RH)	Breakage
Bone, ivory, horn, antler	(low RH)	Splitting/cracking
Old glass	(low RH)	Crizzling, powdering
Composite artifacts (canvas paintings, inlay, skin drums)	(low or high RH)	Warping, cracking delamination
Metal	(high RH)	Corrosion
Certain minerals	(high RH)	Powdering
Paper	(high RH)	Embrittlement
Photographs	(high RH)	Warping, adhesion

with those of the collections. The best we can do is find a compromise that does the least amount of harm to the collections while allowing the museum to function properly and fulfill its mission. To find that compromise, you need to monitor the climate in a meaningful way that helps you understand your particular situation and helps you take steps to achieve the appropriate climate for your collections.

Early museum literature suggests controlling the temperature and RH within narrow ranges according to a single set point. It was also decided (rather arbitrarily) that a flat 50 percent RH at 70°F was the most desirable climate for all museums. In reality, most collections do better in cooler temperatures and somewhat dryer conditions. Current research indicates that most of the damage to artifacts occurs during extremes of seasonal dryness and dampness.[6] Short-term fluctuations are not as important as we once thought because collections take time to equilibrate fully. We really should be keeping the climate for the entire museum within an acceptable RH range (30–60 percent), no matter the season. At the same time, we need to pay special attention to the needs of particular artifacts in the collections that could be greatly affected by adverse climate

The balanced approach

With climate you are trying to balance the cost of maintaining a good climate with the reward of good collections care. Some types of materials are adversely affected by an unstable climate, while others are not affected as much. The real effort should be made to achieve as stable a climate as you can for the artifacts that will be most affected by adverse climate conditions.

Rule of thumb

A neat rule of thumb for RH values is that within the narrow range of temperature typical for museums (65°–70°), for every 1°F of temperature change there is a corresponding change of 1–2 percent RH (depending on the temperature) in the opposite direction. How can you use this to your advantage? If the RH in your storage area is low in the wintertime, you can raise it by simply lowering the temperature. For example, if your storage room has an RH of 30 percent at a temperature of 70°F and you lower the temperature by 5 degrees to 65°F, the RH will rise to around 37 percent.

---

conditions. Composite artifacts made from plant and animal materials (such as skin drums) splitting under low humidity or metals corroding under high humidity are just two examples.

The museum should strive to create a stable climate for the collections. The concept is to create a protective box around the artifact. Sometimes that box is the museum building itself, if it is climate controlled. If it is not, then create a smaller box around the artifact that is climate controlled or at least provides some protection from a rapidly changing climate. This might be a sealed exhibit case with a climate-buffering agent such as silica gel, a sealed storage cabinet, or a sealed plastic container. Even a sealed plastic bag or an acid-free cardboard box with acid-free tissue paper creates a better climate around the artifact than exposure on open shelving. Not all collections are susceptible to damage from an unstable climate, but some are. Good stewardship of collections includes creating the right type of environment for each type of material.

Checklist for Preventive Conservation Strategies

- ✓ Keep track of climate data from year to year to pinpoint problems and track improvements.
- ✓ Identify collections materials requiring special care to prevent damage from an unstable climate.
- ✓ Regularly consult museum literature and other museum professionals to gain a deeper understanding of the effects of climate on collections.
- ✓ Have written collections management procedures that address climate issues in the museum, such as window and door closures, the

temperature of the storage room, and the use of humidifiers and dehumidifiers in the building.

✓ Use computer data loggers to gather climate data and review that data on a regular basis to maintain and improve the climate in the building. Or use inexpensive temperature or humidity instruments to check the climate of your museum.

✓ Build in-house expertise on analyzing climate information or regularly consult outside experts.

FAQ

Question: Our museum is not air-conditioned, so occasionally, in the summer months, doors and windows are opened to provide cooling for our museum. Is this a problem?

Answer: Whereas this activity does promote better human comfort, it increases the risk to the collections. Open windows and doors allow more dust and insects to enter the building, provide quick entry or exit for thieves, and could be left open by mistake after closing. Alternatives should be considered, such as fans to circulate air or limited opening of certain windows during cooler, early-morning hours followed by closing windows and curtains to trap in cooler air. A written policy governing when opening windows is appropriate and what precautions must be taken would help ensure that the collections are protected.

Question: What is the best heating system for our museum?

Answer: That depends on a lot of factors. The real question, though, is how to heat the building in winter and still provide an appropriate climate for the collections. On the whole, we are good at heating to a human comfort level. We often fail to provide enough humidity for the collections while we are heating the building. If your building type permits installation of an HVAC system that adds moisture to the air, this will help create a suitable climate for your collections. Otherwise you will need to look at creating an appropriate climate for the individual artifacts that are susceptible to damage from an unstable climate.

Institutional mind-set

The institution expends enough resources to create a climate that is within an acceptable range and appropriate for the collection.

---

2. Light: Why Is It So Dark in Here?

There are two kinds of light—the glow that illuminates, and the glare that obscures.

—James Thurber

As the curator opened the 1950s vintage cracker tin, the first thing that struck me was the vibrant yellow of one of the balls of wool yarn. The delicate yellow comes from a type of lichen that grows in southeastern Alaska. I had seen it before on the iconic robes worn by indigenous peoples of southeastern Alaska, but never like that. Several other yellow balls from the container were in a separate bag with a tag saying they had been on exhibit. These were a dull version of the one that had remained in the tin. It occurred to me that in traditional ceremonies, robes would have been revealed only for short periods before they were packed away until the next ceremony. Light exposure would have been minimal and the colors preserved. Continual displaying of these artifacts has exacted a high price.

Visible and ultraviolet (UV) light cause significant damage to collections, which generally goes unnoticed until light-sensitive items are quite disfigured. The greatest challenge for most museums is lighting for exhibits. Artifacts require light to be seen, yet light causes damage. This is one of the basic conundrums for museums. How can we light our exhibits and still be good stewards of our collections?

What Is Light?

Light is energy. Specifically, light is electromagnetic radiation transmitted in a wavelength visible to our eyes. UV is a more energetic form of electromagnetic radiation and is invisible to the human eye because it falls below the visible spectrum. Because UV light is more energetic, sources of light in museums that contain UV (especially daylight but also fluorescent bulbs) cause damage more quickly. UV light is not useful in museums and should be eliminated. However, eliminating UV solves only a small part of the equation. Visible light still causes most of the damage to light-sensitive collections. It is therefore important to control the overall light levels in your museum, even if the UV is filtered out.

How Does Light Impact Collections?

Light falling on an item interacts with its surface. The energy of the light is absorbed by the surface molecules, causing them to change. Some of this change manifests as fading, as seen in textile dyes, printing inks, photograph colors, watercolors, and colors on natural history specimens. Other changes can be seen as yellowing or darkening, as seen in resins, varnishes, unpainted wood, and news-

Photo 1.2. After sixty days of exposure to daylight, the dyes on this paper faded. It is important to note that the middle section was protected behind a UV filter. It shows almost as much fading as the far right section, which was unfiltered daylight. (Photo by Sara Boesser)

print, for example. The effects of light on some items can be surprising. Proteins can become brittle after exposure to light and start to break apart, weakening the artifact. Silk, for example, is made of protein produced by the silk worm and loses more than half its strength after only six months of exposure to sunlight. Smoke-tanned leather fades quickly, while certain old glass bottles that were once clear can take on a purplish hue due to the effect of light on the manganese dioxide used as a decolorant in the glass. Traditional oil paintings, on the other hand, are not as susceptible to light damage as one might think, even though they are quite colorful. This is because oil paint is composed of ground pigments (mainly minerals) in a drying oil, which gives them pretty good color retention. This does not mean that you can expose oil paintings to excessive light; you just do not have to be as strict with them as you would with watercolors, which are made from dyes, for example.

Photo 1.3. Fading on textile exposed to too much light. (Photo by Scott Carrlee)

What Can You Do about Light?

The first step is to start taking light-level readings in your museum. This is an essential part of protecting your collections from light damage. Light meters are not very expensive. Many states have field service offices for museums that will loan you one.

In museums, we measure light in foot-candles (fc) or lux. The foot-candle, which measures lumens per square foot, is the more common measurement used

Table 1.2. Effects of Light

Material	Cause	Effect
Dyed textiles	Light affecting dyes	Fading
Paper	Light causes lignin to become acidic	Fading, yellowing, embrittlement
Photographs (especially color)	Light affecting dyes and optical brighteners	Fading, loss of optical brighteners
Smoke-tanned hides	Light affecting color	Fading
Certain minerals	Light affecting color	Fading
Painted surfaces	Light affecting color	Fading
Wood/plant material	Light affecting constituents in material	Darkening
Feathers	Light affecting color	Fading
Colored elements (such as insect parts)	Light affecting color	Fading
Silk	Light affecting proteins	Loss of strength
Plastics	Light affecting constituents	Embrittlement
Old glass	Light affecting manganese	Purple color

Photo 1.4. Taking light readings inside an exhibit case. (Photo by Scott Carrlee)

in the United States. Lux measures lumens per square meter and is part of the International System of Units (commonly referred to as the metric system) used in Canada, Europe, and almost everywhere else. The conversion factor between foot-candles and lux is roughly 1:10—1 fc equals roughly 10 lux—which makes it easy to convert between the two.

A foot-candle is defined as "a unit of measure of the intensity of light falling on a surface, equal to one lumen per square foot and originally defined

---

Rule of thumb

The human eye adapts remarkably to changing light situations. We know it does this by changing the pupil size. In bright light, the pupil constricts to reduce the amount of light falling on the retina; in low light, the pupil expands. The range of acceptable light in museums is 5–30 fc. The lower limit is set at 5 fc because below that level, it is difficult to perceive true color value. What about the upper limit? At 30 fc, the pupil starts to contract and shut light out. Therefore, light levels above 30 fc are really not that useful in the museum setting.

---

with reference to a standardized candle burning at one foot from a given sur-face."[7] This definition tells us one important thing about measuring light. The foot-candle measures the amount of light that actually falls on a surface. This is important because you want to measure the light falling on the artifact, not the light emitted by the light source, to determine the danger to the artifact.

Protecting against UV exposure may require the use of a UV meter. UV meters are expensive, and most small museums do not own one. Again, check with a field services officer in your state to see if you can borrow one. You only really need a UV meter to see if your light sources contain UV or to see if filters are working properly. Once you know your light sources are filtered or the UV has been eliminated, you will not have to use a UV meter again until you change your light source. UV filters are thought to last at least ten years.

Even if you cannot do anything immediately to remedy high light levels, you should at least familiarize yourself with the current levels. The next step is to determine which artifacts are sensitive to light, then to reduce the light on them to an appropriate level. Since light damage is cumulative—meaning the damage builds up over time—even a little bit of light can cause damage if the duration is long. Therefore, you need to look for anything with color and then determine if that color is made from a dye or an ink. Start planning to reduce the exposure for light-sensitive artifacts on display.

Educating your museum visitors about light damage and creating an exhibit space where they feel welcome will increase visitor satisfaction. Upon entering from outside, visitors will need a moment to let their eyes adjust before moving into a gallery with low light levels. A well-lit introductory gallery with text panels and light-stable artifacts is a good beginning. Adequately lit walkways and exhibit text panels will help visitors appreciate the displays. Text labels with larger font sizes and contrasting backgrounds make reading easier. Creating situations where sensitive collections are lit only when being enjoyed by patrons is a challenge but may provide a way to keep light-sensitive items on display for longer periods. Most importantly, you should understand that not all collections are light sensitive. For those that are, however, light damage is cumulative, irreversible, and preventable.

The balanced approach

With light, you are trying to balance visitors' experience with the long-term protection of the artifacts. It is essential to have enough light so the visitor feels comfortable moving around the exhibits. Exhibit text panels must be readable for everyone. It is not so much a question of how much light is in exhibits but rather of where it is falling.

Checklist for Preventive Conservation Strategies
- ✓ Use a light meter to determine the light levels in the exhibit areas.
- ✓ Use a UV meter to check the UV content of the light sources for exhibit and storage. Generally, a reading of below seventy-five microwatts per lumen is acceptable.
- ✓ Use shades and sheers to block daylight from windows.
- ✓ Systematically eliminate all UV in the museum, including daylight and fluorescent sources, through filtering.
- ✓ Move sensitive objects to areas with less light, or move the light source farther away.
- ✓ Adjust lights to appropriate levels where possible, using lower-wattage bulbs or dimmer switches.
- ✓ Rotate light-sensitive objects off exhibit.
- ✓ Use color photocopies in place of light-sensitive printed materials where appropriate.
- ✓ Always turn lights off in collections areas when not in use.
- ✓ Write a lighting policy that sets recommended light levels for all collections on exhibit (i.e., watercolors will only be lit to 5 fc).
- ✓ Inform new employees and volunteers of the importance of reducing light levels to protect objects.

FAQ

Question: I have put UV filters on the windows of my museum. Do I still have to reduce the light levels?

Answer: This is a common question with regard to light levels in museums. UV is only part of the light-damage equation. You do have to consider the overall light levels coming in through the window. Indeed, daylight is much more powerful and damaging to collections because a large portion of its energy falls in the UV range. Eliminating UV through filtration is a good idea and does reduce the damage. However, if the light levels are still high (above 5 fc for the most light-sensitive objects) and the duration is long, then there will be damage even with all the UV filtered out.

Institutional mind-set

The institution is aware that light can cause irreparable damage to its collections. The institution monitors light levels and makes every effort to light artifacts appropriately for their sensitivity level.

Question: I run a historic house museum. We have a lot of daylight coming in through the windows. I have started to notice fading on furniture and some of the textiles we have out. I do not want to block off the windows as that is not how people would have lived back then. What can I do?

Answer: Lighting in historic houses is always a problem. First, you can hang UV filters in the windows. These are sheets of clear plastic that hang (like a shade) on the inside of windows and, if cut to the right size, are barely noticeable. Next, you can use period-appropriate curtains, shears, or shades to block some of the light coming in through the windows. In addition, you should use a light meter to measure light levels at various times of day and during different seasons. You should be able to determine where, in the various rooms, there are darker areas to display light-sensitive objects. As a last resort, use replicas of light-sensitive items, and put the originals in storage.

Question: Our museum budget is tight this year. Our board has asked me to use more energy-efficient light sources. I am considering switching to compact fluorescent lights (CFLs) for the overhead lighting of the exhibit galleries. Is this an okay option?

Answer: Energy efficiency should be a goal of every museum. CFLs will save an amazing amount on the electric bill and are appropriate for certain situations. The caution here is that they do emit a lot more UV radiation than the incandescent (tungsten or halogen) bulbs you are replacing. You should be careful not to use CFLs to light exhibits containing light-sensitive objects. You may be able to save as much energy (and therefore money) by installing dimmer switches for your current lighting.

3. Pests: Critters Eating Collections

> One tiny insect may be enough to destroy a country.
>
> —Arabic proverb

I saw the first ant crawling on the printer in the middle of a desk outside the break room. I did not think much about it as we often see picnic ants in the museum when the weather warms up. Then there was another ant, and another, and another. I could follow a solid line of ants from the desk in the hall to the break room. I suspected spilled sugar or something on the counter, but these ants seemed to be using the break room only as a transit point. The line snaked along the floor molding, ending behind a large storage cabinet. I ripped up the molding behind the cabinet and found a hole in the wall where the ants were pouring in. Now I had the entry point, but why were they swarming all over an office desk? The culprit was some sticky red fruit punch that had run beneath the printer. Someone had cleaned up the mess but neglected to look beneath the bulky printer. The ants were having a party.

All museums have pests. The bad pests are often called "heritage eaters." Even benign pests that are only using the museum for shelter or seeking a food source other than collections can lead to problems in the future. Damage from insects, rodents, and other pests is always a potential hazard for museum collections, no matter where the museum is located. I have been told with confidence that a certain museum did not have an insect problem because it was too cold in the winter. To staff members' surprise, I was able to show damage of artifacts in their exhibit from an insect infestation. Insects in particular have adapted well in interior spaces and thrive in museums.

What Are Pests?

Pests in museums are like weeds in a garden; they are unwanted and cause damage but might be benign or valued in other circumstances. A squirrel might be a welcome sight gathering acorns on the lawn but not when building a nest in the eaves of your historic house. Pests in museums can loosely be defined as living creatures that cause damage to collections. These can take the form of insects, birds, rodents, or other animals. Mice, squirrels, and other mammalian pests cause trouble mainly for historic properties or living history institutions. The problems they create are, for the most part, obvious, and the solutions straightforward. Eliminating their food sources, stopping them from entering

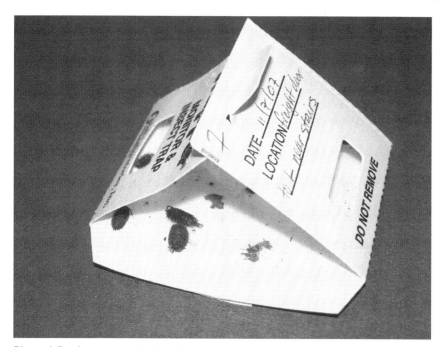

Photo 1.5.   Insects caught in a blunder trap. (Photo by Ellen Carrlee)

15

the building, and trapping will usually keep these pests in check. Insects, on the other hand, are an endemic problem for all museums. They go unnoticed more often than any other type of pests in museums. For that reason, this section will concentrate on insect pests.

How Do Pests Impact Collections?

Insects affect collections primarily by eating them for food. Most are interested in protein- or starch-containing materials, but some are able to digest cellulosic material, such as paper or wood. Pests leave behind evidence of their activities through clipped artifact hair or feathers, holes or bald patches in materials, frass (insect droppings,) bug parts, and cocoons. They may also disfigure surfaces through nests, secretions, and droppings, such as "fly specks." Even insects that do not impact collections directly are unwelcome because they can be a food source for insects that will eventually impact artifacts.

What Can You Do about Pests?

No single magic bullet will rid your museum of all its pests forever. The solution is to manage the problem carefully. The method used by museums today is called integrated pest management (IPM). You should have a written policy that addresses museum pests and includes some form of IPM to protect your collections from this threat.

IPM is a strategy to reduce the number of pests in the museum and the damage they cause by using preventive methods rather than resorting to pesticides, which are now used only as the last line of defense. This was not always the case. Through the first half of the twentieth century, it was quite common to use chemical pesticides on artifacts to kill insects and prevent infestations. In the 1970s and 1980s, coinciding with the advent of scientific research into and conservation of artifacts, museums started looking for ways to control insects without resorting to pesticides.

Table 1.3. Effects of Pests

Material	Cause	Effect
Wood	Wood-boring beetles	Tunnels, flight holes
Textiles (wool, silk)	Protein-eating beetles/clothes moths	Holes, webbing
Leather, skin, fur	Protein-eating beetles	Holes, grazing marks
Feathers	Protein-eating beetles	Holes
Bone, horn, antler	Protein-eating beetles	Holes, tunnels
Paper	Book worm/silverfish	Holes, tunnels
Photographs	Silverfish	Grazing marks
Baskets	Cellulose eaters	Holes

What is IPM?

The agriculture industry developed the concept of IPM as a way of controlling insects and at the same time reducing the amount of pesticides used. The museum field adopted it with the same goals in mind.

The IPM strategy involves four main areas: prevention, monitoring, identification, and treatment. The main points of an IPM system are as follows:

- Stop infiltration of pests. Find and seal or block the entry points.
- Allow food and drink in designated areas only, and keep those areas clean.
- Prohibit live plants and flowers in the building.
- Remove clutter from the storage area and keep it clean.
- Monitor for pests using sticky traps (also called blunder traps) set in strategic locations. Two per room is a good starting point. They should be set along the wall because most insects crawl there rather than out in the middle of a room.
- Check traps regularly and record your observations. Put new traps in the same places as the old ones so that you can detect patterns.
- Identify pests caught in the traps. Websites and cooperative extension offices are good sources for identifying insects.
- Examine incoming collections for evidence of infestation (look for casings, frass, webbing, bug parts, loose hair, holes, and bald patches).
- Bag infested artifacts immediately.
- Freeze-treat infested artifacts.
- Carefully remove any insect debris with tweezers or a vacuum after a freezing treatment to allow for future monitoring.

Rule of thumb

The more robust the IPM is in practice, the better protected the collection will be and the more flexible the museum can be about when and where food is allowed in the museum.

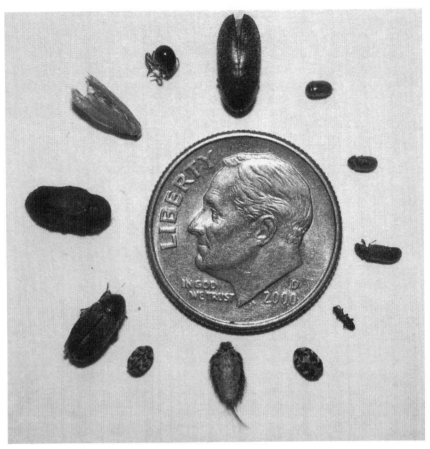

Photo 1.6. Common Heritage Eaters (Photo by Ellen Carrlee)

  1:00 **Cigarette beetle**
  2:00 **Drugstore beetle**
  3:00 **Confused flour beetle**
  4:00 **Saw-toothed grain beetle**
  5:00 **Carpet beetle (black, white, and orange)**
  6:00 **Common carpet beetle larvae**
  7:00 **Varied carpet beetle (black, white and gray)**
  8:00 **Common dermestid beetle**
  9:00 **Larder beetle**
10:00 **Webbing clothes moth (ragged wings)**
11:00 **American spider beetle**
12:00 **Hide beetle (has white underside)**

Freeze-Treatment Protocol

1. All material should be sealed in a plastic bag. The phrase "bag and cuddle" is sometimes used to indicate putting buffering materials, such as acid-free tissue paper, in the bag around the artifact both to control humidity and to protect artifacts during cold-induced brittleness. It might help to place the object on some sort of support.
2. Get as much air out of the bag as possible without crushing the artifact.
3. Place the bag in a freezer (set to its coldest setting).
4. Leave the bag in the freezer for one week.
5. Remove the bag and let it come to room temperature for a day (do not remove the artifact from the bag).
6. Return the bag to the freezer for one week.
7. Remove the bag and allow it to reach room temperature before opening. Objects will be cold and brittle. They are more susceptible to mechanical damage at this point. Handle with care and as little as possible. Condensation may form on the outside of the bag as it warms up. Keeping the artifact in the bag prevents the moisture from damaging the artifact.
8. Clean insect debris from the artifact using tweezers or a vacuum.

Checklist for Preventive Conservation Strategies

✓ Implement an IPM program suited to your museum.
✓ Immediately after events at which food is present, clean the affected areas and remove food-containing trash from the building.
✓ Monitor all incoming collections for pests before bringing objects into collections storage. If in doubt, bag objects until closer inspection or an IPM strategy can be carried out.
✓ Inspect, and perhaps utilize preventive freezing for, all gift shop inventory, workshop materials, and hands-on or educational materials.

The balanced approach

With pest control you are trying to balance resources (staff time, funds) with the actual threat that pests pose to collections. Utilizing IPM to manage your pest problems may appear to return little on the investment but is an essential part of keeping your collections safe.

✓ Remove from the building as soon as possible all packing materials from donations and gift shop inventory.

✓ Do not allow plants and cut flowers in the museum. This should be addressed at the policy level.

✓ Inform new staff and volunteers of the museum's IPM policy.

✓ Check sticky traps quarterly (twice a year may work better for seasonal museums).

✓ Use a floor plan to indicate where the pest traps are set.

✓ Using a spreadsheet helps keep track of what insects are appearing in which area. Certain pests may not affect collections but may indicate excessive moisture or other facility concerns.

FAQ

Question: We are hosting a reception in our museum. Can we allow food at this program?

Answer: It is difficult to eliminate food from museums. They seem to go together like wine and cheese. If you have a good IPM in place, you can probably host a food reception without endangering your collection. You should take extra precautions, such as cleaning and removing food and trash immediately after the event. Food in your museum should be addressed at the policy level. Written procedures should serve to implement the policy.

Question: How often should I check the insect traps?

Answer: It is a good idea to check them on a regular schedule. For most museums, a quarterly basis works best, while for others, like seasonal museums, twice a year at the beginning and end of the season may work better. When you first institute monitoring, you should check more frequently (like once a month) in order to develop a catalog of the insects typically present in your museum. As you begin to understand the patterns, you can dial back to a quarterly basis. Certain circumstances may necessitate more frequent monitoring. Seeing a single suspicious insect is a good reason to put out a few extra traps in that area to determine if you have a resident population. Good times to step up monitoring are when you are bringing in a new collection or changing your food policy.

Institutional mind-set

The institution should be aware that there will always be a pest problem, especially a resident insect population, at the museum.

After an infestation, it will be important to increase the number of traps and the frequency of checking them to make sure that your mitigation efforts have been effective.

Question: Should we use pheromone traps?

Answer: Pheromones, which attract insects to the trap, are not well suited for use in museums. Pheromones are powerful attractants for insects and can actually lure insects into the museum as an unintended consequence. They are also very insect specific, so you need to know exactly what insect you are trying to catch. Only under very limited circumstances should they be used—for example, to trap webbing clothes moths in a sealed storage cabinet.

Question: Can we have plants in our museum?

Answer: Large plants have been known to house mouse nests in the dirt. Dirt is nutritive to molds and insects, especially gnats. Plants are another food and water source for insects. Cut flowers can hide bugs and eggs. Flowers and plants are not compatible with a successful IPM strategy, and this should be addressed on the policy level so that it is understood by all staff and volunteers and does not cause problems.

4. Pollutants: Keeping It Clean

All the king's horses and all the king's men can't put the past together again. So let's remember: Don't try to saw sawdust.

—Dale Carnegie

The exhibit titled "Transportation through the Ages" was a bit out of date. Judging from the bright orange paint in the background and the wood paneling, I would date it to the late 1960s or early 1970s. It would have looked great in the *Brady Bunch* living room. Another giveaway was that the last artifact in the series was a model of the Concorde supersonic jet, captioned "The Future of Commercial Air Travel." Somewhere in the middle of the exhibit was a model of a stagecoach drawn by a team of six horses. The model was intricate, with the reigns and yokes on the horses executed in great detail. The yokes had a problem though: They appeared to be covered with white fuzz. Research indicated that the modeler had used lead to shape the yokes and then painted them to look like wood—this being easier than actually carving small pieces of wood. The problem was that the case's construction materials contained formaldehyde and other volatile organic components (VOCs) that reacted with the lead. Over time, the surface of the lead beneath the paint became covered in white crystals of lead corrosion. This was not the look intended by the model maker or the exhibit designer but rather the result of using exhibit materials incompatible with the long-term preservation of the objects.

Pollutants are easy to ignore as a threat to the collection. The cause-and-effect relationship between pollutants and damage is not well understood by most museum staff. The damage may take a long time to appear on artifacts, and the sources of the pollutants are not always known. In addition, difficulties such as lack of funds, tight schedules, or simple lack of knowledge often lead to poor choices in materials and methods for storing and displaying artifacts. A lot of research has been done in this area over the years, particularly by the British Museum, the Getty Conservation Institute, the National Park Service, the Victoria and Albert Museum, the Boston Museum of Fine Arts, the Smithsonian, and the Image Permanence Institute, just to name a few. It is important to know that pollutants do affect your collections, and certain procedural changes and informed choices can make a difference in protecting your collections from this threat.

What Is Pollution?

Really three forms of pollutants affect museum collections: pollution from the outside; pollution from the inside in the form of volatile organic components, which is commonly referred to as "off-gassing"; and pollution in the form of dust. Pollution from the outside may be man-made (e.g., factory emissions, automobile exhaust) or natural (e.g., volcanic eruption, forest fire). Pollution from the inside usually comes from exhibit construction or storage support material but can also come from cleaners used in exhibits such as glass cleaner. One must pay particular attention to the VOCs in materials used to construct display cases, including wood products, paints and other finishes, carpeting, and so on, because these tend to get trapped in with the artifacts and cause damage over time. Some woods contain acids that will affect collections. Materials used to store collections can also have a long-term effect if not stable. Acidic high-lignin paper or unstable yellowing plastics are examples.

Dust should be one of your main concerns because it is ever present and difficult to remove completely from the museum environment. It can cause damage to artifact surfaces and especially to natural history specimens. Therefore, effective collections care requires good housekeeping. Dust has many sources. Some

Why does dust adhere so well to the surface of artifacts?

Dust contains a large percentage of bacteria. These living entities go about living and dying and excreting in order to create an environment that promotes more bacterial growth. Eventually the buildup becomes a well-adhered layer on the surface of the artifact.

regions or museum types will have more of a problem than others. Historic properties located in the countryside might deal with dust from a gravel or dirt road. City traffic can produce excessive dust in museums. Visitor traffic is also a main source of dust in museums.

How Do Pollutants Impact Collections?

Collections exposed to pollutants and VOCs can tarnish, corrode, discolor, or become brittle. Acidic window mats used to frame artwork can cause what is called mat burn. You see this most clearly when the old mat is removed from the artwork. An obvious line of yellow or brown near the bevel-cut edge of the mat is caused by volatile acids from the acidic material inside the mat.

Certain pollutants affect metals in particular. Sulfur causes silver to tarnish by forming silver sulfide. Sources for sulfur in an exhibit case could be wool in exhibit textiles or backing cloth or rubber gaskets on the exhibit or storage case itself. Formaldehyde causes lead to form white powdery corrosion on the surface by forming lead formate, as does acetic acid, which causes the formation of lead acetate. VOCs mostly affect artifacts with metal components.

Dust is sometimes mistakenly thought of as benign; yet artifacts exposed to a lot of dust will look dull and ratty over time. Feathers are particularly vulnerable because the small barbules trap dust, which can cause them to deteriorate more quickly. Dust contains abrasive particles that can cut and scratch on a microscopic level. Dust attracts moisture, promoting corrosion as well as biological growth, such as mold and bacteria. Bacterial colonies excrete waste products that adhere dust to surfaces, making it more difficult to remove.

What Can You Do about Pollutants?

It is difficult to eliminate pollutants completely from the museum environment. Good filtration on the HVAC system (if you have one) will cut down on some of the pollutants and dust entering the building, as will keeping windows

Table 1.4. Effects of Pollutants

Materials	Cause	Effect
Metals	VOCs	Corrosion
Protein-containing materials (fur, feather, skin, leather)	Dust, VOCs	Brittle, breakage, loss
Artifacts with fragile surfaces	Dust	Difficult to clean
Photographs	Dust	Embeds in surface
Framed prints, drawings, and watercolors	Acidic window mats	Mat burn
Unvarnished paintings (acrylic)	Dust	Surface grime
Taxidermy specimens	Dust	Dull surface

and doors closed. More importantly, making good choices as to what types of display and storage materials are used will keep potentially damaging VOCs away from sensitive artifacts. Check online sources or the National Park Service's *Exhibit Conservation Guidelines* for appropriate materials. Replacing acidic window mats with acid-free/lignin-free museum board is a good example of a measure any museum can take to eliminate one damaging source of pollutants. This would make an excellent grant project.

Good housekeeping helps keep dust down. Regular cleaning of exhibit cases and collections on open display is essential to protecting the collection from this threat. Usually, cleaning exhibits once a year (before the tourist season for seasonal museums) is enough to promote good collections care. The best way to dust off collections on exhibit is with a high-efficiency particulate air (HEPA)–filtered vacuum. The HEPA filter traps very fine particles of dust and prevents them from being blown around the museum. It is best to use HEPA vacuums on which it is possible to turn down the suction when cleaning artifacts of dust. A soft paintbrush designated for dusting only should be used to brush the dust gently toward the nozzle of the vacuum. It is also useful to secure some plastic window screening over the nozzle of the vacuum to prevent any small parts from inadvertently being sucked up. Hold the nozzle away from the surface, sucking the dust out of the air as it is fluffed loose with the brush.

Sealed exhibit cases help keep dust out in the first place and reduce the amount of dusting that is necessary. However, sealed exhibit cases could trap VOCs inside, causing damage to artifacts. Thus, it is important to use low-VOC materials in exhibit case construction.

With very few exceptions, bagging artifacts in open storage (i.e., not in sealed storage cabinets or boxes) promotes better longevity than leaving them exposed. Bags not only protect from pollutants like smoke, soot, or dust but also provide a more stable climate, limit damage from handling, help contain possible detached pieces, limit the extent of an infestation, and protect objects from water. Use polyethylene plastic bags that self-seal or use a heat sealer. If you are heat-sealing, leave enough extra bag so that it can be resealed when necessary. I have seen collections that have been in bags for more than thirty years, and they are in great condition. The benefits far outweigh any worries you should have about bagging artifacts. The exceptions are wet or damp artifacts or those that are inherently unstable. Wet or damp artifacts will get moldy. It is important

---

Rule of thumb

Under most circumstances, cleaning the dust from exhibits once a year is probably enough to maintain an appropriate level of care for the artifacts.

> **The balanced approach**
>
> With pollutants, you are trying to balance staff time and museum resources with how much damage can occur. A generally clean and tidy museum overall and a staff that is aware of the appropriate materials for the storage and display of artifacts is the goal.

to make sure artifacts are dry before bagging. As a general rule, if an artifact is stored in a normal museum storage room (i.e., interior space, heated in the winter), it will be dry enough to bag without problem. Unstable artifacts, such as those containing cellulose nitrate, give off volatile components as they deteriorate. These can build up inside the bag and speed deterioration in a vicious cycle.

Checklist for Preventive Conservation Strategies
✓ Write a housekeeping plan.
✓ Regularly clean exhibits using a HEPA vacuum.
✓ Build new exhibit cases in accordance with the National Park Service's *Exhibit Conservation Guidelines*.
✓ Use inert materials from reputable suppliers for storage and exhibits.
✓ Place all artifacts on open storage shelves in boxes or plastic bags.
✓ Use polyethylene bags (recycle code 2).

FAQ
Question: Some of my exhibits are difficult to access for dusting. Would it not be better just to leave well enough alone?

Answer: Not really. It is important that all artifacts included in permanent collections receive the same general level of care. It would be a good idea to start working toward making the exhibits easier to clean. Cleaning those difficult areas every other year would be better than not cleaning at all.

Question: One of our volunteers is a woodworker and wants to build us a new exhibit case. I know you have to be careful about what kinds of materials go into the case. Is there a list I can check somewhere?

Answer: The National Park Service has done a great deal of work in this area and has produced a CD titled *Exhibition Conservation Guidelines*. Some common mistakes are using plywood and leaving wood exposed. If possible, use coatings and building materials that are labeled as low VOC. Covering wood with paint or varnish helps reduce off-gassing from the wood but does not prevent it completely. Remember, coatings of any kind need adequate time to cure before collections are placed inside.

> **Institutional mind-set**
>
> The institution should strive to keep the museum clean and tidy. A clean museum promotes good collections care.

5. Human Interaction: Handle with Care

> They're funny things, Accidents. You never have them till you're having them.
>
> —Eeyore, *Pooh's Little Instruction Book*, inspired by A. A. Milne

The beautifully engraved silver punchbowl with walrus motifs complete with ivory tusks was a repeat visitor to the conservation lab. It was on loan to a historic mansion that put the bowl in harm's way more often than it should have. Unauthorized holiday floral arrangements were wearing away the delicate gold wash inside. The first treatment was to remove fingerprints etched into the surface by improper handling. The next was to repair a tusk that broke when the punch bowl slid off a piano during a move. The final straw was the leaky drainpipe that had dripped raw sewage into it. The solution (other than to recall the loan, which could not happen for political reasons) was to build a custom exhibit case that made the bowl accessible only to museum staff.

Human interaction is a broad category of threats at the interface where people and artifacts come together. Human interaction can cause irreversible damage to collections or complete loss through theft or negligence. Artifacts that are not properly protected from visitors (i.e., those on open displays) are particularly vulnerable. Yet even well-trained museum staff can also cause damage to collections through accidents, neglect, well-intentioned but misguided cleanings and other treatments, and consumptive use. The phrase "consumptive use" may not be universally familiar; it refers to museum activities involving the object (i.e., hands-on educational programs, sampling, operation of mechanical artifacts) that result in loss, part replacement, weathering, or

> **The Paradox of Washington's Axe**
>
> Discussions of consumptive use bring to mind the paradox of Washington's axe. The story goes that a museum was offered the original axe that George Washington used to cut down the cherry tree. Of course, over the years the handle had worn away, so it was replaced, and the head had rusted away, so it was replaced as well. But it still occupied the same space as the original.

wear and tear. Of all the threats, human interaction impacts collections most frequently and most universally.

What Is Human Interaction?

Any time people and objects come together, there is the potential for damage. If an object is locked away in a vault, there is not much chance it will be damaged by human interaction. However, collections exist to help fulfill the institutional mission. This presents another museum conundrum: Using collections helps the museum to fulfill its mission to interpret and educate, but public trust duty requires the museum to care for collections in perpetuity. To be effective stewards of the collection, a museum needs to go beyond simply striking a balance between protecting collections and educating its audience (which would imply compromising some on each); it must do both well.

How Does Human Interaction Impact Collections?

The impact on collections from human interaction can range from incremental damage to total loss. An artifact is most vulnerable during certain transitional phases and when it is accessible to the public. The transitional phases include initial processing, preparation for exhibit or loan, cleaning or conservation treatment, and the occasional move into new storage. Damage

Photo 1.7. Poor storage conditions lead to damage. (Photo by Ellen Carrlee)

> **Rule of thumb**
>
> Gloves should always be worn when handling collections. There are very few exceptions to this rule. It is especially important to wear gloves whenever handling objects with the public present. This sends the right message about collections care.

from the public occurs primarily when collections are on exhibit. This is when the public has the opportunity to touch or pick at an item. When collections are in an appropriate storage situation or incorporated into an exhibit that follows conservation principles, they are generally safe from the threat of damage from human interaction. They are in a preservation environment.

It is hard to list all the types of collections affected by human interaction because the list basically includes all collections. If something can be lost, stolen, broken, scratched, dented, torn, and so forth, it is susceptible to this type of damage. The collections most likely to incur handling damage are those that are most fragile. The collections most likely to be stolen are those that have monetary or collectable value or are most accessible. Really, however, all collections are affected.

Photo 1.8. Fingerprint permanently etched into silver plating. (Photo by Ellen Carrlee)

Table 1.5.   Effects of Human Interaction

Cause	Effect
Inappropriate handling	Buildup of grime, yellowing, breakage
Theft	Total loss
Vandalism	Damage
Loss	Total loss
Incorrect packing for shipping	Breakage
Opportunistic touching while on exhibit	Buildup of grime
Poor exhibit mounting techniques	Scratches, dents
Improper storage and overcrowding	Surface damage, deformation
Poor or nonexistent storage supports	Scratches, more handling
Inappropriate sampling	Loss of significant portions of the artifact
Consumptive use	Incremental loss of the artifact
Inappropriate restorations	Irreversible damage
Inappropriate cleaning	Surface damage

What Can You Do about Human Interaction?

Thinking ahead is the best way to prevent damage caused by human interaction. No aspect of damage caused by human interaction is unpreventable. It is basically a question of risk management. Managing risk requires developing a philosophy of care that pervades the institution. The basis for managing this risk rests in a museum's policies and procedures. While some policies and procedures might seem to be commonsense or understood, it is important that everyone who works with collections is on the same page. What is common sense to one person might not appear on someone else's radar. Thus, there should be a written policy and written procedure for all activities that involve collections (see chapter 4 in this book for more information). There is a difference between policies and procedures, and it is important to understand and keep the two separate.

Policies clearly establish the standards that regulate the museum's activities. They identify what needs to be done and provide a framework to help staff make decisions. Policy statements are approved by the governing authority. Procedures tell staff how to do things and provide the mechanism and details for implementing the policy. Procedures are a series of succinct and unambiguous action steps that are developed at the staff level. They do not have to be approved by the governing authority.[8] Simply put, policies are what need to be achieved and procedures are the nitty-gritty of how to get there.

Checklist for Preventive Conservation Strategies
✓ Address issues of human interaction on the policy level.
  ◦ A lock or key policy governs who has keys to what areas.
  ◦ A handling policy governs who handles objects and what training is needed.

- ○ An access policy governs who has access to what areas.
- ○ A security policy governs issues involving the security of objects.
- ○ An exhibits policy establishes principles for preparing and exhibiting artifacts.
- ✓ Implement good handling protocols in the form of written procedures for when artifacts are handled and where they are kept safe during collections processing and exhibit preparation.
- ✓ New staff, volunteers, and interns should receive training on how to handle objects and the expectations for working in collections and around objects.
- ✓ Be aware of preexisting conditions that might make artifacts more vulnerable to handling damage, such as age, previous mends, or cracks and other damage.
- ✓ All artifacts should be moved on carts.
- ✓ Prevent direct contact between collections and the floor to protect objects from kicking and tripping as well as water damage and soiling.
- ✓ Use pencils in collections areas (instead of pens). Pencil marks are easy to remove; pen marks are nearly impossible to remove.
- ✓ Utilize cases and vitrines to protect objects on exhibit.
- ✓ Be especially careful of dioramas with small objects on tabletops and the like. These are prime situations for damage or theft.
- ✓ Use stanchions or plinths to keep objects physically out of arm's reach while on exhibit.
- ✓ Place "Do not touch" signs where objects are vulnerable to touching on exhibit.
- ✓ Replace vulnerable objects on exhibit with replicas.
- ✓ Keep the gift shop separate from exhibit areas.
- ✓ Make hands-on opportunities, including interactive exhibits, look different from your regular exhibits. Distinguishing between the two reduces confusion for museum visitors.

The balanced approach

With human interaction, you are trying to balance access to the collection with preservation of the collection. If you never allow anyone near your collection, there is less of a chance that something will get damaged because of human interaction. But allowing no access to collections is not going to help your institution achieve its mission. Therefore, we must be able to allow access but still protect the collections.

Institutional mind-set

The institution should take a cue from the medical profession. It would stand out if certain ways of doing things in a hospital were not followed, like wearing a mask while performing a surgery. Similarly, appropriate behavior should be maintained around objects in a museum. Collections should always be in a safe location, whether in storage, on exhibit, or on loan. Objects should never be on a cluttered table. Gloves should be worn when handling collections. One should never be rushed when handling objects. These kinds of practices go a long way toward keeping artifacts safe.

FAQ

Question: I just started working as the director of a small museum. No one seems to know who has keys to the front door, but I know that several longtime volunteers and at least one former director have keys. What policy should we have in place about locks and keys?

Answer: A good key policy is one that works for your institution. The important thing is to have one and to make sure that it is approved and signed by your governing authority. Limiting who has off-hour access to your museum is important for protecting the collections. There is a high incidence of insider theft at museums. Having checks and balances and a limited number of keys that access collections protects the collection as well as the integrity of the staff.

Question: At the historic house museum where I work, some of the staff members encourage visitors to turn the crank of an old ice-cream maker or stand on the back of a dogsled because it makes history more "real." They often say, "This stuff was meant to be used!" How can I make my point that this behavior could cause damage in the long run?

Answer: This gets into the question of consumptive use of collections. Certain collections can be used for demonstration purposes. These are usually called educational or programmatic collections. It is important to note that artifacts in these collections are very different from artifacts in the permanent collection. Permanent collections are held in the public trust to be cared for in perpetuity. Therefore, consumptive use is not appropriate for them. All museums should make good, reasoned decisions as to what goes into each type of collection. Questions to ask yourself and your institution include the following: Is the item rare? Does it have a good background story? Did it belong to an important person in the community? Can it be easily replaced? By taking these things into consideration, you can make an informed decision about what can and cannot be used.

Question: Do I really need to wear gloves if I am only moving something quickly?

Answer: Handling something with bare hands will always leave some evidence of that interaction, usually in the form of oil. It may be imperceptible at first, but over time it will show. Consider how briefly you touch a light switch and how quickly the switch plate becomes grimy. I make it a point always to handle artifacts with gloves on. It is just a good habit to get into. I notice that people are more focused when they wear gloves. There is also the issue of not knowing what contaminants (e.g., mercury, arsenic, mold, lead dust) are on the artifact. You are protecting yourself as well.

6. Disasters

Plans are useless, but planning is indispensible.

—Dwight D. Eisenhower

The water fountain was right outside the basketry storage vault, and of course it started to leak on a Friday evening, after the museum was closed and everyone had gone home for the weekend. By the time Monday morning rolled around, the water was lapping up to the bottom shelf of baskets. The first people on the scene started handing out the baskets in bucket-brigade style to get them to higher ground. After being handed out, the baskets were placed on empty shelves just outside the vault. But when those filled up, they were placed anywhere they would fit, including on the hallway floor. When they finally arrived with the wet-dry vacuums, maintenance workers could hardly make it through the chaos. We were very lucky that no baskets were kicked or crushed. It would have been better to find an appropriate space before moving any of the baskets. Live and learn!

When a disaster strikes, the thing that will be really useful is not the plan itself but having made it. A response to a disaster is usually a seat-of-the-pants operation that deals with developing conditions on a moment-by-moment basis. The better you have prepared, the more successful you will be in dealing with the chaos that inevitably develops as the situation unfolds. With the basket vault situation, it would have been wise to make (or follow) a plan before reacting.

What Is a Disaster?

A disaster is an emergency that has outstripped your ability to cope. With a good emergency response plan (ERP) and some basic supplies in place, your

What is ICS?

The Incident Command System (ICS) is one of the most essential tools in your disaster-mitigation toolbox. Using ICS will help with the biggest problem that arises during the actual mitigation of an emergency: knowing whom to go to for instructions. To understand the ICS system fully, you will need to read a manual or go online to take a free course. Basically, you put someone in charge, you make that person stay in a fixed location, you assign tasks to competent people, and you cover all your bases (money, supplies, personnel, communications, media, etc.).

emergency, hopefully, will not reach the level of disaster. The most essential part of your ERP should, first and foremost, look after the safety of patrons and staff. Nothing is worth injuring yourself or endangering others for. After all safety concerns are met, ERP is all about keeping the damage to collections to a minimum.

How Do Disasters Impact Collections?

ERPs take into account everything from volcanoes to terrorist attacks. But a disaster will most likely affect collections, in terms of potential for occurrence, through water. Most small-scale emergencies that affect collections involve water, from pinhole leaks in pipes to clogged roof drains. Even in the event of a fire, there will be water damage from efforts to put that fire out.

Types of Collections Most Affected

All types of collections are affected by disasters; however, some materials are more vulnerable than others, particularly because they can be damaged by water.

Table 1.6. Effects of Water Disasters

Material	Cause	Effect
Paper	Water	Running inks
Photos	Water	Sticking together
Wood	Water	Swelling
Paintings	Water	Shrinkage of canvas, lifting paint
Textiles	Water	Dyes bleeding
Metals	Water	Corrosion
Natural history specimens	Water	Matting fur

What Can You Do about Disasters?

Be prepared! The more prepared you are for any emergency, the less of a disaster you will have. This is easy to say but sometimes hard to do. Here are some steps to take to start moving in the right direction:

1. Have basic materials on hand. Since water is the most likely cause of damage, have supplies at the ready that help mitigate water. A wet-dry shop vacuum dedicated to disaster recovery is essential. Plastic sheeting and duct tape will help keep water off unaffected collections. A roll of clean newsprint to interleave between book pages and pieces of paper is very useful, and rolls of paper towels will do in a pinch. Limited storage space will be a factor in how many emergency response materials can be kept on hand. It will be useful also to keep a brief list of where supplementary supplies can be bought or borrowed in a hurry.

2. Write an ERP that takes into account the most likely disasters and the special needs of the museum collections. If it seems you cannot tackle the plan all at once, break it down into smaller parts. Creating a simple phone tree of whom to call in what order is a good start. You can also use online resources such as dPlan (www.dplan.org) to help create your ERP. Once the plan is in place, make sure that copies are available at various locations throughout the facility and that you have at least one copy off-site in a secure location.

3. Assessment of risk can help prioritize other collections care needs. Storing collections in boxes or bags can save thousands of hours of work since replacing wet boxes or bags is far easier than treating wet collections.

4. The plan should be updated on a regular basis. It is good to have some mechanism to encourage the updating of the plan. An annual event in conjunction with the national preparedness month (September) will help keep your plan current. Discussing current events for the museum at every staff meeting will keep people aware. Simply touching on the weather, who is on vacation, and construction in and around the museum will keep emergency response on staff members' minds.

As a general rule, most people's first impulse is to start picking up artifacts and moving them out of the affected area. I believe that the shock of seeing

> **The balanced approach**
>
> With disasters, you are trying to balance the resources required to stay pre-pared with the costs associated with not being prepared.

precious artifacts at risk makes us want to do something immediately. For the most part, this is not the best plan of action. The sequence should be as follows:

1. Make sure no one is in danger or will be placed in danger by remaining in the area.
2. Stop whatever is causing the problem, if possible.
3. Look for a space large enough to accommodate the impacted collections.
4. Move those collections.

Generally, when collections are wet, soot covered, burned, or otherwise affected during the emergency, the damage has already been done. Very little good comes from hurrying collections to the wrong space, only to find they are in the way and must be moved again. A thoughtful, planned move is best in almost all cases.

You should make every effort to acquaint yourself with your local emergency responders. Invite them over for a tour of your institution. Make sure they have a floor plan of your museum and are aware of special collections or circumstances, such as hazardous chemicals. Discuss with them how a response would be carried out, and make sure they are aware of your concerns. Give them a copy of your ERP. These relationships will be very helpful when an emergency occurs. You should consider taking the online course on the basic Incident Command System (ICS) offered on the Federal Emergency Management Agency's website (www .fema.gov). All trained emergency personnel, such as firefighters and police, use the ICS system to handle emergencies. If you are familiar with the language of the ICS, you are more likely to be included in their response decisions. ICS can also help you organize your response to any disaster, no matter how small. It is a good system for implementing the command structure for a response.

Checklist for Preventive Conservation Strategies

✓ Have a written ERP (approved by the governing body) that covers these essential areas:
  ○ Personal safety
  ○ Emergency-specific action steps

Photo 1.9. Water-damaged archives storage box caused by a leak in the roof. (Photo by Damon Stuebner)

Rule of thumb

Since water is involved in many emergencies, mold can quickly create serious health consequences for those providing the response in your mitigation efforts. Since mold likes to grow in warm, moist, dark, and still environments, you should strive to create the opposite environment. You should keep the lights on, the heat off, and fans blowing until you can dry out the area where the water is. Generally, RH under 70 percent and temperature under 70°F should inhibit mold growth. According to the Image Permanence Institutes Preservation Calculator, it takes mold 163 days to germinate under those conditions. Raise the RH to 85 percent, and there is a risk of mold growth in only six days.

- Emergency phone numbers, whom to call first, and who calls whom (phone tree)
- Basic mitigation for collections
✓ Discuss the plan on a regular basis with staff (at the end of staff meetings).
✓ Practice the plan in a tabletop fashion.
✓ Create a mechanism for keeping the plan up to date.
✓ Discuss the plan with local emergency personnel (firefighters, police).
✓ Run a full-scale scenario once per year.
✓ Have supplies on hand or list where they can be obtained quickly (i.e., floor fans rented or large tables borrowed).

FAQ

Question: I work at a small museum with only two employees and a dozen volunteers. Do I really need to learn the Incident Command System?

Institutional mind-set

The institution should make emergency planning part of an ongoing discussion among staff. It would be effective to share a few thoughts on emergency response at the end of every staff meeting. Just mentioning things such as weather, seasons, building repairs, and staff members on vacation will help to keep response on people's minds.

Answer: The ICS is designed to scale to any size emergency response. No matter what the emergency is, you will always need to provide some sort of effective response, and that response will include some sort of command structure, even if it merely entails volunteers coming to you and asking what they can do to help. ICS just gives a formal structure to the process. Using the principles of ICS even in the most basic form will help you respond to an emergency more effectively. It is also helpful to know ICS because your local emergency responders will be using it. Knowing ICS will help you to integrate with that response.

Question: We have been trying to write our disaster plan for years, and it never seems to get done. What should we do?

Answer: This is a common problem for small institutions where no one has the time to write the plan. Turning to online resources might help you get started. You could send a staff member to a workshop where writing the plan is part of the outcome. You can write a grant to contract out the job. If nothing else seems to work, break the plan down into smaller chunks. A simple phone tree for whom to call in an emergency is a good start. Creating a simple flip chart of each potential disaster for your institution is not that hard. You should start with this as a baseline minimum.

Conclusion

It is a myth that we can stop deterioration of collections. Conservators talk about restorations or stabilization treatments, but I believe it would be a mistake to interpret these phrases as final solutions, like putting the artifact into some sort of suspended animation. The artifact is still deteriorating. The question is simply how long it will take for the artifact to deteriorate to the point where it is no longer of value to the mission of the museum.

We can exert some influence on this process and prevent much of the damage that will occur in the lifetime of the artifact. In this respect, we should really be thinking in terms of "deterioration management." Decay will not be solved at one time or with one event. Instead, we must continually manage the problem to ensure the best outcome for our collections and our museums. Through thoughtful measures we can stop preventable damage from occurring. Creating a preservation environment can also slow the chemical breakdown of artifacts. We may not be able to stop deterioration completely, but through the prudent use of resources, we can eliminate many causes of damage.

Deterioration management is like risk management: both attempt to mitigate the impact of potential events. Looking at the six areas outlined in this chapter, you can see that not all risks are equal. Some, like a disaster, may never occur under your watch. Preparation and preventive measures can mean that disasters or other emergencies, if they occur, will have less impact on your collections. However, it has been my experience as a conservator working in museums that human interaction causes the most damage of all the factors reviewed in this chapter. The interface where people interact with the collections—be it protecting them from the public while on display, processing them for storage, packing and shipping them, or handling them for research purposes—creates the highest potential for damage. It pays to put a lot of resources into mitigating this source. This is where you will get the most bang for your buck. Good policies and procedures that determine who interacts with your artifacts, as well as when, where, and how, will do the most to protect them. Creating an institutional mind-set and a method of operation, including good collections management and exhibit practices that promote safe human interactions with collections, is at the forefront of deterioration management.

Further Reading and Resources

This section provides some resources for gathering more information on each of the topic areas of this chapter. Rather than provide an exhaustive bibliography, I thought it would be more useful to provide a must-read list of three references (a book, an article, and a website) for each topic covered above. All of these resources are readily available and particularly suited for the small museum.

Climate

Lull, William P. *Conservation Environment Guidelines for Libraries and Archives*. Ottawa: Canadian Council of Archives, 1995.

Reilly, James. "Specifying Storage Environments in Libraries and Archives." Paper presented at the symposium "Gray Areas to Green Areas: Developing Sustainable Practices in Preservation Environments," University of Texas, Austin, Texas, 2007. Available at www.ischool.utexas.edu/kilgarlin/gaga/proceedings.html.

"Environmental Management: Overview Statement." Image Permanence Institute. www.imagepermanenceinstitute.org/environmental/overview.

Light

Cuttle, Christopher. *Light for Art's Sake: Lighting for Artwork and Museum Displays*. Oxford/Burlington, MA: Butterworth-Heinemann, 2007.

Patkus, Beth Lindblom. "Protection from Light Damage." In *Preservation of Library and Archival Materials: A Manual*, edited by Sherelyn Ogden. 3rd ed. Andover, MA: Northeast Document Conservation Center, 1999.

"Damage and Decay." ReCollections. http://www.collectionsaustralia.net/sector_info_item/3.

Pests

Florian, Mary Lou. *Heritage Eaters: Insects and Fungi in Heritage Collections*. London: James & James, 1997.

Carrlee, Ellen. "Integrated Pest Management Made Easy." In *Alaska State Museums Bulletin* 29 (winter 2007): 1, 3. Available at www.museums.state.ak.us/documents/bulletin_docs/bulletin_29.pdf.

Museum Pests. www.museumpests.net.

Pollutants

Hatchfield, Pam. *Pollutants in the Museum Environment*. London: Archetype Publications, 2002.

Carrlee, Ellen. "Dust in Museum Exhibits." *Alaska State Museums Bulletin* 30 (fall 2008): 1, 3. Available at /museumbulletin.files.wordpress.com/2011/01/bulletin-30.pdf.

"Dust and Decay." ReCollections. http://www.collectionsaustralia.net/sector_info_item/3.

Human Interaction

Odegaard, Nancy. *A Guide to Handling Anthropological Museum Collections*. Los Angeles: Western Association for Art Conservation, 1991.

U.S. National Park Service. "Chapter 6: Handling, Packing, and Shipping." In *Museum Handbook, Part I: Museum Collections*, 1–30. Washington DC: National Park Service, 2007.

Museum Security Network. www.museum-security.org.

Disasters

Heritage Preservation. *Field Guide to Emergency Response*. Washington, DC: Heritage Preservation, 2006.

U.S. National Park Service. "Hazardous Materials Health and Safety." *Conserve O Gram* 2/1. July 1993. National Park Service. www.nps.gov/museum/publications/conserveogram/02-01.pdf.

Museum SOS. www.museum-sos.org.

Notes

1. Marie C. Malaro, *A Legal Primer on Managing Museum Collections*, 2nd ed. (Washington, DC: Smithsonian Institution Press, 1998), 406 and 19.

2. Malaro, *A Legal Primer*, 19.

3. See the AAM website at www.aam-us.org.

4. See the AAM website at www.aam-us.org.

5. James Reilly, *Specifying Storage Environments in Libraries and Archives* (paper presented at the symposium "Gray Areas to Green Areas: Developing Sustainable Practices

in Preservation Environments," University of Texas, Austin, 2007), 3. Available at www.ischool.utexas.edu/kilgarlin/gaga/proceedings.html.

6. Reilly, *Specifying Storage Environments*, 4.

7. "Foot-candle," Dictionary.com, 2004, http://dictionary.reference.com/browse/foot-candle (accessed December 28, 2009).

8. John Simmons, *Things Great and Small: Collection Management Policies* (Washington, DC: American Association of Museums, 2006).

STRAIGHT TALK ABOUT HISTORIC STRUCTURES AND LANDSCAPES

Bruce Teeple

Three hundred years ago, a famous philosopher opened himself to eternal ridicule by declaring this "the best of all possible worlds." That fellow obviously never worked in a small historic house museum. You know better. You are always straddling two or three worlds. One moment, you are doing research to fine-tune your site's interpretation; ten minutes later, you are unclogging a toilet. Do not forget the chamber of commerce meeting in an hour and that busload of school kids arriving this afternoon.

Not only has another saying—"The road to hell is paved with good intentions"—withstood the test of time better than your building and grounds, but it also accurately describes their history. You are discovering that your well-meaning predecessors ignored preservation fundamentals and settled for inappropriate Band-Aids. One person's thrift is another person's irresponsibility.

Resourcefulness is in your blood, but no one wants to be at the mercy of mystery. Should you take Jolly Jerry's Hardware up on its discounted exterior paint? The price is tempting. While you suspect the colors are not historically inaccurate, you are not alone in finding them aesthetically repulsive. To compound the problem, not only is Jolly Jerry on your board of directors, but his brother is a landscaping contractor who offers services and prices that sound too good to be true.

Visitors and potential donors get their first and most lasting impressions from a site's buildings and grounds. How long will your collection last if that roof or window leaks wind and water? The ivy on your wall lends atmosphere, but you remember reading something about vines harming structures. You cannot expect visitors to have pleasant memories of your facility if they trip over a broken sidewalk.

We tend to take for granted the not-quite-visible magic wands waved by our technological society. Walls and wires, pumps and pipes go through the same cycles of birth, growth, decay, and resurrection as any tree, porch, antique loveseat, or curator. Each has its unique appeal; yet their futures are intertwined.

Some suggest it is too expensive or restrictive to maintain your historic house museum responsibly. Others say that rehabilitating the property as a commercial space may be more effective. You, your staff, and your board of directors believe differently, though. None of you wants to betray your community's trust and belief in your ability to showcase a history for the future.

Whether full-time, part-time, or volunteer, you work in a small museum. That means, according to the definition of the American Association for State and Local History (AASLH), your annual budget is under $250,000. You want to spend your time, energy, and money prudently to preserve the place for future generations.

Communication and expertise are crucial. Reputable contractors appreciate working with customers who are familiar with their trade's terminology and conversant about problems and remedies. This chapter reviews issues and ways workers in small historic house museums can establish practical priorities while adhering to basic preservation standards.

Changes

Sometimes conflicts arise when we equate "historical" with "unchanging." Has your historic house museum learned how to embrace and adapt to change? Change is not a threat; it is an opportunity to grow and create new cultures of decision-making. Museums are not cemeteries; only tombstone epitaphs are written in stone. Vibrant, dynamic historic house museums adopt plans and policies that are responsive and resilient to changing circumstances.

For over twenty years, seismic changes in philosophy and attitude toward historic property management have radically revised site interpretations. By excavating and restoring exteriors and landscapes according to acceptable standards, you can tease out even more stories about how the grounds and structures were used. It is perfectly legitimate to show both how structural changes met the occupants' changing demands and how they reflected changing definitions of beauty and utility. Ideally, we can tie it all in with the surrounding community's history.

Change can also affect the mind-set running your operation. Institutions all across society are exploring alternative ways to make decisions. Authoritarian, hierarchical chains of command are yielding to more inclusive, interwoven circles of participation and responsibility. "That's not my job" becomes "It is everyone's job."

Governing bodies need to commit themselves seriously to a progressive strategic plan that welcomes input from everyone on everything: from servicing boilers to controlling foot traffic, from installing light filters to planting flowers. These all have a part to play in telling your site's story. It does not make much sense to preserve your interior collections properly if the structures housing them are dilapidated or your grounds are not welcoming.

Do your house museum's policies and actions encourage alternative ways of learning and does seeing the ripple effects change perceptions? Design adaptations, such as wheelchair ramps, lower water fountains, and Braille signage, for example, have broadened our sensitivities. The same applies to our understanding of how the indiscriminate spraying of wide-spectrum pesticides on lawns and gardens degrades the environment.

Even the most mundane task, such as recycling, has multiple social benefits. Simply placing well-marked bins or cans in strategic locations not only shows a better way to do things but also encourages resource conservation and spreads good will among the wider community. Integrated pest management techniques also make sense by working with nature, saving money, and serving as selling points to potential donors.

Since identity is a powerful tool, structures and landscapes may work together as a symbol, but they should always impart a unique sense of place. Historic house museums only have as much value as their stewards give them. They are often called their community's crown jewel, but jewels need polishing and a proper setting if they are to last.

So, in what direction is your small historic house museum going?

Sustainability

The historic house museum community anticipated the twenty-first century eight years early when it published a new philosophy known as the New Orleans Charter.[1] Too many institutions spent inordinate amounts of money and energy vainly trying to grab the brass rings of accreditation and listing on the National Register of Historic Places.

Graduate schools teaching a one-size-fits-all approach often ignored a community's fragile webs of nuance, connection, and memory. This often resulted in mediocre research, conformist expectations, and museums alienated from their communities.[2]

Other historic house museum administrations were spinning on a hamster wheel, guided by an erroneous definition of "museum quality." As one critic notes, the term comes from the art world and "assumes aesthetic quality" at the expense of a historic house's appropriate "historical or scientific context."[3]

The charter jettisoned older theories stressing rigid principles and began to emphasize flexible, graduated standards. Historic house museums gradually abandoned marketing models based on heritage tourism. Sustainability through education and community service has since become the operative theme.

The General Lew Wallace Study & Museum in Crawfordsville, Indiana, for example, used its CAP and MAP recommendations to conduct successful fundraising efforts at both the local and national levels.

New, inexpensive programs, such as AASLH's Standards and Excellence Program for History Organizations, are pioneering approaches in self-evaluation by incorporating concepts in sustainability. The American Association of Museums' Museum Assessment Program (MAP) and Heritage Preservation's Conservation Assessment Program (CAP) are more traditional but just as beneficial.[4] (See chapter 1 in Book 1 of this series for more information about these programs.) Outside funding sources appreciate the wisdom of this idea and now look more favorably on institutions with sustainable action plans.[5]

It is understood that structures and landscapes will absorb the biggest part of your budget. Buildings and grounds communicate their needs in a different language, but they are still part of your collection. Honest and credible efforts to preserve them and to educate and reach out to the community will speak for themselves. Your small museum's strength comes from balancing the needs of your collections, buildings, surroundings, visitors, and neighbors. The place to start is with your mission statement.[6]

Mission Statements

If you do not have a mission statement, everyone connected with and interested in your museum's operation needs to sit together and create one. It should concisely articulate the meaning of your activities, what you want to promote, and how you plan to do it. Maintaining your assets does not comprise the mission; they are tools to help make it possible. While the quality and quantity of the information a museum visit conveys are important, the information itself does not stick with a visitor the way impressions of the experience do.[7]

If you have a mission statement, when did you last look at it? Personnel, boards, technologies, and communities always change, so it is a good practice to review and possibly revise your mission statement every five years. The mission statement is a guide to help you determine priorities and courses of action. Everyone connected with your museum should be aware of it. Whenever anything confronts you, your board, or your staff, you should have a culture in place where the first response is, "Does this support the mission?" A good mission statement is the key: It is your referee, your insurance policy, your anchor to reality, your grip on sanity, and your lifeline to the community.

Assess the Situation

Before you do anything, you and your board need to become familiar with preservation issues. Read background information provided by your local and state historic preservation agencies, the National Park Service's Preservation Assistance Division, and the advisory council of Historic Preservation. (See the resource list at the end of this chapter for specific reading recommendations.) That way you are prepared to ask and answer questions that arise during the next step: soliciting professional advice. Your mission, your credibility, and your future all hinge on following the Secretary of the Interior's Standards for Preservation.

You also need to assemble an interdisciplinary team of professionals to assess your museum functions.[8] One study will review each structure's condition (historic structure report). Another will recommend ways to fit your landscape's highlights into the visitors' total museum experience (cultural landscape report).

You will learn what is needed to balance human use with the preservation needs of your buildings and grounds. With your mission as your guide, you can decide what practices are appropriate in supporting education, preservation, and accessibility.

Historic Structure Report

The historic structure report will require you to inventory all your assets. Photographs, blueprints, and drawings of everything will help in identifying and documenting what makes (or made) your place's history unique, distinctive, and significant. If there were additions, you may want to bring in an expert in nail analysis to pinpoint the various construction periods of the extant structure. The following list of issues, while not comprehensive, gives an idea of what to look for in your initial inspection.

- *Hazards:* Look for the most obvious hazards. For example, you should take certain precautions before removing lead paint, such as preventing chips and dust from contaminating the ground. Broken pipe insulation poses another problem. Not only is it ineffective but it may also have asbestos-containing materials, the effects of which only properly licensed contractors and trained workers can abate.
- *Electrical use:* How is your electrical system? All wire coverings dry out and crack over time. Knob-and-tube wiring once did a fine job of delivering electricity, but that was also when, and why, electric bills were called light bills. Whether you have a sixty-, one-hundred-, or two-hundred-amp service, a licensed electrician can tell you what amperage will accommodate changing needs. If a

microwave, computer, leaf blower, battery chargers, and appliances all share the same circuit, you need to eliminate that fire hazard by installing more receptacles. The same goes for extension cords; they are for temporary, not semipermanent or permanent, use. All outdoor connections should be fitted with ground-fault circuit interrupters to prevent shock or electrocution.

- *Architectural design:* Primary sources, if available, can tell you what significant changes—fires, demolitions, additions—have occurred since the place was built. They may even offer clues about any missing design elements, the materials used, and how and why uses of a house wing changed. This study will also help you determine how current and future uses, such as parking lots and bus turnarounds, will have the least negative impact on the buildings and premises. With your mission statement as your guide, you will be able to decide if restrooms, offices, and meeting areas are better located outside the house or if you can blend them with the building's unique design.

- *Conservation and preservation:* Energy audits conducted by your local utility company can uncover ways to save on heating and cooling costs. It may pay to investigate alternative energy sources that reduce water and electrical use. That dripping faucet and those cracked windowpanes will not fix themselves, nor are they consistent with your mission's desire to conserve resources and keep within appropriate preservation guidelines.

- *Code compliance:* Your assessment team will also determine the load-bearing capacities of your floors, so you can plan for future uses. A five-thousand-pound printing press should not rest on a floor that can only handle three thousand pounds. And things would not go well if you held a banquet for one hundred people in a third-floor room with an occupancy rating for fifty. Adequate on- or off-site storage space for artifacts or extraneous items, such as tables and chairs, is one way to ease the stress placed on carrying capacities. The historic structure report will show what your facilities need to do to comply with Americans with Disabilities Act regulations. Restrooms, elevators, entrances, and walkways are all considered here. In addition to the state and federal laws, you will also have to comply with local codes and ordinances.

Houses and related structures do not exist independently; they are parts of an integrated whole that includes the surroundings. They all have answers to the same questions. The challenge is to bring them together seamlessly.

Cultural Landscape Report

Landscaping is more than just trimming trees, planting flowers, and mowing grass. The landscape itself is an artifact and therefore a valid teaching tool. Your landscape can tell as many stories about change as your house and its contents do. Members of your staff, board, and the public may all suggest ways to interpret your surroundings. Your cultural landscape report consultants will show you how to channel that energy and enthusiasm appropriately.

It is also recommended that you refrain from any outdoor excavation until you have conducted a thorough archaeological survey of your entire site. You can choose from a smorgasbord of technologies—from ground-penetrating radar to aerial photography to radio-controlled "moles"—with a range of costs.

Maps and drawings, many corroborated by records you or others may have, will help. To grasp and manage the concepts of space and time, the report may divide your site into sections or zones. The names of those areas—Hortense's Herb Garden, the Magic Maze, or the Path of Inspiration—become reference points in planning and helping the visitor see connections.

You will need to decide on your landscape's focus period or periods. Your house may have been built in 1760 with parts added in 1860, but as far as you know, the garden only dates to 1960. The flowers and shrubs you ultimately choose should stay true to the period of your mission's focus.

Soil layers can reveal stories as intriguing as those told by artifacts found in archaeological excavation. Over yonder is a slightly circular dip in the ground. Grass there with differently colored soil and texture may be evidence of a tree having once stood in that spot. If you are lucky, there may be a stump from which you can determine its age by counting tree rings, a discipline known as dendrochronology. An expert in seed or pollen analysis may also be able to identify old crop sites such as vegetable plots, fruit trees, or vineyards.

The cultural landscape report will not be limited to your site's past; planning for present and future use is equally as important in fulfilling the mission. There are practical design matters to consider, such as locating parking lots and maintenance sheds, ensuring adequate drainage, and arranging refuse storage.

Think of it as learning how to play according to Mother Nature's rules when deciding what activities are permitted where. If you plan to use certain areas excessively—for instance, to hold a summertime concert series on a lawn—you may want to plan ways for that area to rebound. The materials lining driveways and walkways will have different characteristics and effects. Concrete sidewalks would be no more appropriate along a hiking trail than having visitors track wood chips or loose gravel into your facility.

Maintenance and renovation work are not done at night by elves. There is no reason to keep all this work on your structures or surroundings away from the

> Time and money will be two of the biggest factors affecting your decisions. At Magnolia Grove and Gaineswood in Greensboro, Alabama, the outside assessor established priorities, ranking them in urgency from 1 to 3. Priorities were also given expense rankings of $, $$, or $$$.

public's view or awareness. People do not mind change as long as it is positive. Some may also like to see how and why decisions are made, so feel free to share all work with your visitors, either on-site or on your website. This process, while seemingly unfamiliar or even onerous, can become a vital part of your visitors' overall museum experience. Do not forget that you are fulfilling the mission by balancing human use with nature through education.

From Hippocrates to Spike Lee, one message echoes through the ages to stand as a guiding principle: Do no harm by doing the right thing. Once your historic structure and cultural landscape reports have identified your problems in those areas, you need to develop a strategy to resolve them. Any responsible homeowner would perform the same tasks listed here. The only difference is that your actions revolve around a mission emphasizing education and sustainability.[9]

Not everything has to be done yesterday. You may be able stretch some jobs over several years. The main thing is to set your priorities. In your first year, you will want to inspect the premises thoroughly before creating an action plan tailored to your specific financial and logistical situation.

Action Plan for Historic Structures and Landscapes

Take It from the Top: Roof and Chimney

After reviewing any records you have of past work, you will begin your historic structure and cultural landscape inspection by looking at the roof and planning for its inevitable replacement. Depending on your climate, consider scheduling an inspection on a semiannual or at least annual basis. You will first look for stains underneath the roof or along the interior walls. Check for soft,

> **Getting Started**
>
> Carry a pocket-sized spiral tablet with you at all times. Write notes to yourself whenever you walk the grounds and around the structures. As a general rule of thumb, try to do the worst first, whenever you can.

cracked, rotted, or blistered areas. Look with binoculars, either from the ground or through windows, if doing so will help you see things from a better angle.

Note the flashing around the chimney, vents, and dormers. These are prime areas for leakage problems. If you need to recaulk, use a marine-quality or silicone latex brand. You may need to replace individual slates, tiles, or shingles, especially if the contractor did not use aluminum or galvanized roofing nails or screws. Look at the roof's low edge. It should form a continuous line and extend three-quarters of an inch or more beyond the edge.

People may not have been concerned with insulating a roof or wall in the day when firewood supplies seemed inexhaustible. Insulation today makes sense, stays within preservation guidelines, and fulfills your mission. As long as roof insulation remains dry, uncompressed, and properly ventilated from soffit to peak, you will save considerably on your heating and cooling costs and prevent dangerous ice dams from forming on your roof.

Every roofing material has it own characteristics. Slate is heavier than most materials, but it can last over a century, as long as you check for loose shingles and weak flashing points. Clay tiles are as durable as slate, but you will need to monitor and attack moss, algae, and lichen growth. Wooden roofs only last half as long as clay tiles, but similar fungus problems can plague them too. Metal roofs have the longest life spans, ranging anywhere from twenty to one hundred years, depending on the quality of the material and the climate. Asphalt shingles, the most common material, usually have the shortest lifetimes, from fifteen to twenty-five years.

While you are checking the roof, see if weather vanes, antennae, or snow guards and brakes are fastened tightly. If the chimney is out of plumb, you will need to have a mason straighten it. Water infiltration poses the biggest potential problem, but most masonry, if maintained properly, will last many years. Under no circumstances, however, should you consider cleaning masonry surfaces by sandblasting them. The process does irreparable harm.

Do not use more than one heating unit, no matter what it is, per flue. If your heating units are hooked into a chimney, you will need to repoint cracked, broken, or missing mortar joints as soon as possible. If your mason is relaying or repointing older, softer brick, make sure he avoids using mortar mixes with Portland cement; they are too hard and will crack the brick.

It's All about the Drainage

When you are checking out the roof before and after winter, inspect and clean the gutters at the same time. You might consider investing in leaf strainers and guards to eliminate the need to perform this unpleasant but necessary task. Make sure the hangers are not loose or causing storm water to flow away from

> **Caution**
>
> Preservationists discourage any open fires in and around historic structures. Please consider sealing off all fireplaces permanently, since fireplaces lose more heat than they produce. Mission fulfillment, not superfluous atmosphere, is your goal. If you insist on burning wood in that fireplace, make sure that the flue has a terra-cotta liner, that the wood has thoroughly dried for at least a year, and that you schedule a professional chimney cleaning annually.

downspouts. Flush the entire drainage system with a strong jet from a garden hose twice a year.

Where does your water go? Water flies off a roof edge faster and in greater and more concentrated volumes than if the roof were not there. The leading cause of damp or flooded basements is roof runoff. The bottom piece of spouting should curve outward to divert water from the foundation, onto a splash block, and preferably into a collection system. Make sure the grade slopes away from the building to ensure proper drainage.

How Firm a Foundation

Your foundation should be as solid and tight as your financial picture. You need to seal foundation cracks. Insects, water, and rodents are all equally adept at finding these entryways. The building itself should rest at least eight inches above the grade to discourage insects and to prevent water from splashing up on vulnerable surfaces.

Stained or discolored masonry and wooden walls may indicate a condensation problem. You can remedy that with either adequate ventilation or with 6-mil polyethylene vapor barriers. Crawl spaces, porches, and steps should have vents six inches above the grade. Position vents five feet from every corner, with a minimum of twenty-five feet between them. Any wood in contact with the soil will encourage termite infestations, so it is advisable to replace that soil with concrete.

The Inviting Package

Your exterior walls, windows, and woodwork make one of the most lasting impressions on visitors. The twice-yearly inspection route should look for stained or buckled siding, a sure sign of condensation, rot, or bugs. Caulk the ends of wooden pieces or places where dissimilar materials meet, such as windows, doors, or foundations. Bugs and water will also exploit these weak spots.

Air needs to circulate around your structure. Remove all nearby leaf and rubbish piles, and trim back any branches that inhibit airflow. The same goes for vines, such as ivy. They not only penetrate the smallest openings and rip out mortar joints but also make it impossible to paint.

Plan to paint wooden surfaces every five to seven years. If done well, though, a good job will last twice as long. If you need to replace any rotted wood, talk with your preservation consultant first. Keep a record of paint colors, if possible. Avoid applying oil paints on latex or vice versa. As mentioned earlier, you will also need to test your old paint for lead content. Whether you decide to encapsulate or remove lead-based paint, it is a hazardous process, so contractors must take certain precautions to ensure the safety of both workers and visitors.

Window inspection and cleaning should occur at least once a year. Replace cracked panes to prevent air infiltration. Seal or replace defective sills. Settling foundations may make it difficult to open windows and doors. Cracked jambs and warped thresholds should also be repaired as soon as possible.

The Lay of the Land

The earth and its flora operate on a different time frame than humans, so landscape inspections and evaluations are only necessary every three years. The cultural landscape report has inventoried and mapped all plant life on the property to determine what is appropriate to the mission, so now is the time to begin acting on its recommendations.

Table 2.1. Types of Building Damage

Where?	When?	Look For	How to Fix
Roof	Semi-annually	Stains/loose shingles/flashing	Caulk or replace as needed
Chimney	Semi-annually	Water infiltration/worn, broken or cracked bricks	Repoint joints or replace bricks as needed
Gutters	Semi-annually	Loose hangers/blockages/reverse flow of water	Flush with hose before and after winter
Foundation	Semi-annually	Cracks/signs of condensation/wood in contact with soil	Seal all cracks; only concrete should be in contact with soil
Siding/woodwork	Annually	Stains/rot/buckling/plant growth against building	Scrape; paint; repair or replace as needed; remove plant growth
Windows/sills/jambs/thresholds	Annually	Cracks/misalignment	Repair or replace as needed

Discuss your plans with reputable consultants and contractors. Do not sacrifice historical integrity by letting contemporary aesthetics rule your decisions. Your responsibility is to be mindful of the mission. Your landscape consultant will offer ways to construct service facilities, visitors' centers, and public walkways without adversely affecting scenic views or disturbing environmentally sensitive areas.

Let the land and the period of your focus talk to you. Eighteenth-century kitchen gardens did not have hybrid vegetables or flowers. Historic or mature trees and native shrubs add an element of grandeur, as long as weak or aged limbs do not raise liability or safety concerns. Try to incorporate the growth of smaller, younger trees into the long-term plan for a given area. Your consultant can suggest ways to control vehicular and foot traffic patterns by positioning plants and beds.

Lawn-care practices have undergone major revisions over the years. Ask local landscape contractors how frequently you should mow the grass, how high to set the blade, and whether to bag and compost the clippings and tree leaves or let them rot in place. Environmentally sustainable practices vary, so your individual situation will determine the questions you ask and the decisions you make.

If you choose a gas engine over an electric one, keep in mind that four-stroke cycle engines have lower emissions and better fuel efficiency than two-stroke engines. Regular repairs and tune-ups according to the manufacturer's specifications ensure cleaner-running engines and keep within the mission too.

Some places wrestle with the idea of even mowing the grass. One alternative, if you have the resources, is to bring sheep, horses, chickens, or peacocks onto the property to control different areas. You will have to research whether their presence is appropriate, humane, or even legal. You will also need to provide sufficient housing for these animals and find proper ways to dispose of manure. Other related issues will concern whether they will be tethered, fenced, or allowed to run free.

If you have outdoor faucets for watering plants, make sure they do not drip constantly. Wet ground and puddles encourage infestations of mosquitoes and other undesirable insects.

Wooden fence posts, trellises, and planters should stand on a concrete footer rather than touch the ground directly. Plants growing near or on them should permit adequate air circulation around nearby buildings.

Maintenance routines should also include monitoring and trimming any tree or shrub growth that touches the building or inhibits air movement. When reviewing work quality, make sure workers prune properly and conservatively. Cuts should be outside the branch; stubs encourage infection and insects.

Cast-iron fences are attractive and extremely durable. Your annual maintenance plan should ensure that all hinges and latches are lubricated. After sandblasting rust and loose paint from these surfaces, applying a new layer of paint every five to seven years will help the fence last for generations.

Look at your signage and how it communicates your mission. The wording for any sign should be clear, concise, and consistent. It also helps if you explicitly state the reason for a particular policy in terms of the mission.

More places are realizing the untapped value of recycling water running off the roof. Barrels or underground cisterns are excellent places to store this water until needed. Your consultant can offer some suggestions for incorporating this concept into a site-appropriate design.

To ensure safety, all maintenance chemicals, tools, hoses, and power equipment should be secured in a sufficiently large storage building.

Responsibilities

Board of Directors

Governing bodies are legally responsible for carrying out their fiduciary duties, delegating authority, and establishing ethical policies. These include avoiding any semblance of a conflict of interest (so much for Jolly Jerry and his brother) and ensuring that all actions adhere to acceptable preservation guidelines.

Board members should meet with the staff, an attorney, and an architectural consultant every five to ten years to review any completed work and to plan for future projects. They should also have either a line item in their budgets or a fund set aside specifically for large jobs and emergencies.[10]

Staff Duties

Effective directors act as a liaison between the board and the staff, making each side aware of the other's actions through monthly and annual reports. They formulate procedures that follow through on the board's policies. These include instructing all parties on the site's history and on sustainable preservation tech-

Board involvement varies from organization to organization. The White County Historical Society in Carmi, Illinois, has an extraordinarily active board with strong ties to the community's movers and shakers. One member reports that the board merely has to send letters or publicize the society's immediate needs through the local radio station and newspaper. Both media outlets are acutely aware of the society's needs because the board puts representatives on various committees.

niques, as well as establishing emergency procedures and contact lists. As part of their emergency training, all staff members need to know the locations of all gas, water, and electrical shutoffs.

With any historic preservation work, maintaining digital and paper trails is required. And when performing any site evaluation, you will need to provide all documentation substantiating arguments about your site's significance.[11] Keep original legal documents—deeds, titles, easements, environmental regulations—in a safe, secure location. You should keep all permanent records and digital copies of what makes your site outstanding and unique, including the date of construction, who built it, a list of the original buildings and trees, and how it all has changed.

The same practice holds true for all maintenance decisions and actions: document everything. All work orders should clearly state, in a consistent format, what specifically needs to be done. Keep records and daily photographs of all work and resources—from National Park Service preservation guidelines to Occupational Safety and Health Administration standards, to your lawn mower's owner's manual, to oral history transcripts, to daily diaries of roof replacement. Keep notebooks on every major project as well as one with your annual preventive maintenance schedule.

You are obviously not doing the actual work; that is performed by a licensed, reputable contractor who understands those particular needs outlined by your preservation consultant. Your most important action, though, is to keep a record of anything concerning roof work (or any maintenance work, for that matter), including date of installation, materials used, colors or brand names used, warranties, contractor's name, workmanship, and estimated replacement date. Think of any questions your successors may ask the next time this work is scheduled.

Regardless of how haphazard this documentation was in the past, now is the time to be thorough and methodical. Documenting the history of change at your site is a legitimate part of fulfilling your mission. Leave nothing to chance. File hard copies in a safe location, and store digital copies so they are all readily available for immediate access by everyone.[12]

When reporting monthly or annually on the state of your site, mention what went into deciding what work was done, what still needs to be done, when the work should be scheduled, and how you will pay for it. Provide invoices and receipts for everything.

As the staff at the Moffatt-Ladd House & Garden in Portsmouth, New Hampshire, discovered, fully documenting their needs and priorities made it easier to obtain grants to pay for the work.

These and many other questions will arise as you plan and decide what projects to defer and fold into future plans. It is all part of the ongoing process of evaluation.

Evaluation

Do not worry about pursuing someone else's ideal vision of a museum. You have read the completed reports on your structures and landscapes, stayed within the mission's focus, and acted to the best of your abilities.

Tweaking and improving the effectiveness of your operations, programs, and interpretations is a never-ending process. Mission statements are not meant to be perfect and eternal. They are human constructs only kept alive and breathing through your efforts. By their very nature, they need to respond to changing realities. Annual, three-year, and five-year plans and evaluations are good ways to measure how effectively you have carried out the consultants' recommendations and fulfilled your mission.

Regard your self-evaluations as pats on the back, but keep your perspective. They are not rocking chairs; they are spurs to action. They help you with charting your energy savings, with developing realistic budgets, and with fundraising efforts.

National Register of Historic Places

How many times has someone told you he plans to have his home or museum listed on the National Register of Historic Places? Both the National Register—a division of the federal Department of the Interior and the National Park Service—and the National Trust for Historic Preservation have been active for decades in promoting preservation, saving properties, and revitalizing communities. These few paragraphs are only intended as a quick reference for answering queries.

Perhaps it is best to look at this subject from the standpoint of preservation rather than prestige. Local, state, and federal groups that recognize historical importance do not want to discourage people from saving old buildings. They want to ensure sustainability by asking whether a community is demonstrating a long-term partnership and commitment to the property's future. They also want to see the site's decision-makers ethically committed to following accepted standards, guidelines, and best practices.

Many misperceptions float around about qualifying for a National Register listing. One of the most common is that the Secretary of the Interior will automatically list a site because the house is old. Longevity, by itself, is hardly a sufficient argument. Other applicants believe they will get on the list merely because they have completed the paperwork. Another misleading idea is that the government will pay for all the necessary renovations.

The National Register uses a variety of criteria in acknowledging a property, including its cultural significance, its unique architectural features, or its past ownership by a noteworthy person. Some key words used in reviewing a house or property are "quality," "significance," "architectural integrity," and "context." Your chances will improve if the property is more than fifty years old or is part of a wider complex, such as a historical district. This list is not comprehensive, and meeting a combination of these criteria will not guarantee your success. You can find a complete listing of the National Register's criteria at the National Park Service's website.[13]

You can save a lot of time and energy, though, by looking into similar programs with tax incentives offered by city or state historic-preservation agencies. Whatever direction you choose, be sure to seek the advice of a professional who specializes in preservation issues.[14]

Conclusion

As mentioned at the beginning of this chapter, dreaming about a distant "best of all possible worlds" is not realistic. Good stewardship is an ongoing process; it is timeless and holistic. Take comfort in knowing that, while the work is never done, you have had a hand in charting a better, sustainable path toward the future for your small historic house museum.

The resources listed in the bibliography are invaluable and authoritative. If all goes well, your structures and landscapes will last many lifetimes.

Acknowledgments

Andrea Malcomb, Molly Brown House, Denver, CO
Eleanor Cunningham, Magnolia Grove and Gaineswood, Greensboro, AL
Marjorie Fechtig, White County Historical Society, Carmi, IL
Larry Paarlberg, General Lew Wallace Study & Museum, Crawfordsville, IN
Heather Quiroga, Historic Denver, Denver, CO
Jeremy Risen, French Lick West Baden Museum, French Lick, IN
Max Van Balgooy, National Trust for Historic Preservation, Washington, DC
Barbara M. Ward, Moffatt-Ladd House & Garden, Portsmouth, NH

It is worth checking out Historic Denver. This group has been in the forefront of using preservation awareness to build a sense of community for over forty years.

Resources

National Park Service Preservation Briefs (www.nps.gov/hps/tps/briefs/presbhom.htm): If you e-mail your requests to nps_hps-info@nps.gov, please include your mailing address. They will send up to five of the following publications free of charge:

- #1—*Assessing Cleaning and Water-Repellent Treatments for Historic Masonry Buildings*
- #2—*Repointing Mortar Joints in Historic Masonry Buildings*
- #3—*Conserving Energy in Historic Buildings*
- #4—*Roofing for Historic Buildings*
- #5—*The Preservation of Historic Adobe Buildings*
- #6—*Dangers of Abrasive Cleaning to Historic Buildings*
- #7—*The Preservation of Historic Glazed Architectural Terra-Cotta*
- #8—*Aluminum and Vinyl Siding on Historic Buildings: The Appropriateness of Substitute Materials for Resurfacing Historic Wood Frame Buildings*
- #9—*The Repair of Historic Wooden Windows*
- #10—*Exterior Paint Problems on Historic Woodwork*
- #14—*New Exterior Additions to Historic Buildings: Preservation Concerns*
- #16—*The Use of Substitute Materials on Historic Building Exteriors*
- #17—*Architectural Character—Identifying the Visual Aspects of Historic Buildings As an Aid to Preserving Their Character*
- #19—*The Repair and Replacement of Historic Wooden Shingle Roofs*
- #20—*The Preservation of Historic Barns*
- #21—*The Preservation and Repair of Historic Stucco*
- #26—*The Preservation and Repair of Historic Log Buildings*
- #27—*The Maintenance and Repair of Architectural Cast Iron*
- #29—*The Repair, Replacement, and Maintenance of Historic Slate Roofs*
- #30—*The Preservation and Repair of Historic Clay Tile Roofs*
- #31—*Mothballing Historic Buildings*
- #32—*Making Historic Properties Accessible*
- #35—*Understanding Old Buildings: The Process of Architectural Investigation*
- #36—*Protecting Cultural Landscapes: Planning, Treatment and Management of Historic Landscapes*
- #37—*Appropriate Methods of Reducing Lead-Paint Hazards in Historic Housing*
- #39—*Holding the Line: Controlling Unwanted Moisture in Historic Buildings*
- #42—*The Maintenance, Repair and Replacement of Historic Cast Stone*
- #43—*The Preparation and Use of Historic Structure Reports*
- #45—*Preserving Historic Wooden Porches*
- #47—*Maintaining the Exterior of Small and Medium Size Historic Buildings*

National Park Service Preservation Tech Notes (www.nps.gov/history/hps/tps/technotes/tnhome.htm):

- Exterior woodwork
  - #1—*Proper Painting and Surface Preparation*
  - #2—*Paint Removal from Wood Siding*
- Masonry
  - #1—*Substitute Materials: Replacing Deteriorated Serpentine Stone with Pre-Cast Concrete*
  - #2—*Stabilization and Repair of a Historic Terra Cotta Cornice*
  - #3—*Water Soak Cleaning of Limestone*
  - #4—*Non-destructive Evaluation Techniques for Masonry Construction*
- Metals
  - #1—*Conserving Outdoor Bronze Sculpture*
  - #2—*Restoring Metal Roof Cornices*
  - #3—*In-kind Replacement of Historic Stamped-Metal Exterior Siding*

Related Readings on Structures

American Association for State and Local History (AASLH). "Technical Leaflets." www.aaslh.org/leaflets.htm. This series was originally published in *History News*.

- #15—*Paint Color Research and Restoration* (1968)
- #48—*Nail Chronology As an Aid to Dating Old Buildings* (1968)
- #67—*Before Restoration Begins: Keeping Your Historic House Intact* (1973)
- #77—*Wood Deterioration* (1974)
- #80—*Historic Landscapes and Gardens: Procedures for Restoration* (1974)
- #89—*History of a House—How to Trace It* (1976)
- #105—*Historic Houses As Learning Laboratories* (1978)
- #132—*Collecting and Preserving Architectural Records* (1980)
- #171—*A Holistic Approach to Museum Pest Management* (1990)
- #173—*Historical Archaeology As a Tool for Researching and Interpreting Historic Sites* (1990)
- #180—*The Americans with Disabilities Act of 1990* (1992)
- #199—*Historic Landscapes and Gardens: Procedures for Restoration* (1997)
- #242—*DIY Strategic Planning* (2008)
- #244—*How Sustainable Is Your Historic House Museum?* (2008)

George, Gerald. "Historic House Museum Malaise: A Conference Considers What's Wrong." American Association for State and Local History. www.aaslh.org/images/hhouseart.pdf.

Morton, W. Brown, III, Gary L. Hume, Kay D. Weeks, and H. Ward Jandle. *The Secretary of the Interior's Standards for Rehabilitation & Illustrated Guidelines for Rehabilitating Historic Buildings.* Washington, DC: U.S. Department of the Interior, 1992.

National Trust for Historic Preservation. *A Layperson's Guide to Preservation Law: A Survey of Federal, State, and Local Laws Concerning Historic Resource Protection.* Washington, DC: National Trust for Historic Preservation, 2008.

———. "America's Historic Sites at a Crossroads." *Forum Journal* 22, no. 3 (spring 2008).

———. *Basic Preservation: What Every Board Member Needs to Know*. Washington, DC: National Trust for Historic Preservation, 2005.

Skramstad, Harold. "An Agenda for American Museums in the Twenty-First Century." *Daedalus: Journal of the American Academy of Arts and Sciences* 128, no. 3 (summer 1999): 109–27.

Vaughn, James. "Introduction: The Call for a National Conversation." *Forum Journal* 22, no. 3 (spring 2008): 5–9. Available at www.preservationnation.org/forum/spring-2008.

Related Readings on Landscapes

Birnbaum, Charles A., ed., with Christine Capella Peters. *The Secretary of the Interior's Standards for the Treatment of Historic Properties with Guidelines for the Treatment of Cultural Landscapes*. Washington, DC: U.S. Department of the Interior, 1996. Available at www.nps.gov/history/hps/hli/landscape_guidelines/using.htm.

Brophy, Sarah S., and Elizabeth Wylie. *The Green Museum: A Primer on Environmental Practice*. Lanham, MD: AltaMira Press, 2008.

Coffin, Margaret, and Regina M. Bellavia. *Guide to Developing a Preservation Maintenance Plan for a Historic Landscape*. Rev. ed. Boston: Olmsted Center for Landscape Preservation, National Park Service, 1998.

Jackson, John Brinckerhoff. *A Sense of Place, a Sense of Time*. New Haven, CT: Yale University Press, 1994.

———. *Discovering the Vernacular Landscape*. New Haven, CT: Yale University Press, 1984.

Lawliss, Lucy. "Preventive Conservation and the Historic House Landscape." In *Preventive Conservation for Historic House Museums*, edited by Jane Merritt and Julie A. Reilly, 117–24. Lanham, MD: AltaMira Press, 2010.

McClelland, Linda Flint, J. Timothy Keller, Genevieve P. Keller, and Robert Z. Melnick. "Guidelines for Evaluating and Documenting Rural Historic Landscapes." National Park Service, 1999. www.nps.gov/NR/publications/bulletins/nrb30.

Stevens, Rebecca. "Preventive Conservation and the Historic House Structure." In *Preventive Conservation for Historic House Museums*. Edited by Jane Merritt and Julie A. Reilly, 125–48. Lanham, MD: AltaMira Press, 2010.

Stilgoe, John. *Common Landscape of America, 1580 to 1845*. New Haven, CT: Yale University Press, 1982.

———. *Outside Lies Magic: Regaining History and Awareness in Everyday Places*. New York: Walker and CO, 1998.

National Register of Historic Places

Before you do anything, contact your state and local historic preservation offices at www.cr.nps.gov/nr/shpolist.htm to become aware of state or local preservation laws that may affect you.

For NPS Bulletin 16, "How to Complete the National Register of Historic Places Registration Form," visit www.nps.gov/nr/publications/bulletins/nrb16a. The National Park Service has a wealth of materials on the National Register program and the Federal Historic Preservation Tax Credits at www.nps.gov/nr/publications/index.htm, including the following:

- Auer, Michael. *Preservation Tax Incentives for Historic Preservation* (2010).
- Bruechert, Daniel. *Introduction to Federal Tax Credits for Rehabilitating Historic Buildings—Main Street Commercial Buildings* (2007).
- Creveling, Elizabeth A. *Introduction to Federal Tax Credits for Rehabilitating Historic Buildings—Barns* (2007).
- Parker, Jennifer C. *Introduction to Federal Tax Credits for Rehabilitating Historic Buildings—Wood Frame Buildings* (2007).
- Staveteig, Kaaren. *Federal Tax Incentives for Rehabilitating Historic Buildings: Annual Report* (2009).

See also Historic Denver's "Owner's Manual for Historically Designated Homes" at www.historicdenver.org/uploaded-files/Brochure_Final%20Draft.pdf. This group and its site provide an excellent template for those museums looking to develop partnerships with their communities.

Notes

1. "New Orleans Charter," Association for Preservation Technology International (APTI), www.apti.org/resources/charters.cfm. This joint document, produced by the American Institute for the Conservation of Historic and Artistic Works (AIC) and the APTI, was adopted by the National Conference of State Historic Preservation Officers.

2. Gerald George, "Historic House Museum Malaise: A Conference Considers What's Wrong," American Association for State and Local History, www.aaslh.org/images/hhouseart.pdf; James Vaughan, "America's Historic Sites at a Crossroads," *Forum Journal* 22, no. 3 (2008): 5–10.

3. Harold Skramstad, "An Agenda for American Museums in the Twenty-First Century," *Daedalus: Journal of the American Academy of Arts and Sciences* 128, no. 3 (summer 1999): 112.

4. You can find more information on these programs at the websites of the AASLH (www.aaslh.org), AAM (www.aam-us.org), and Heritage Preservation (www.heritagepreservation.org).

5. Larry Paarlberg, e-mail, March 14, 2011.

6. "How Sustainable Is Your Historic House Museum?" Technical Leaflet #244, included in *History News* 63, no. 4 (autumn 2008), www.aaslh.org/documents/TL244Autumn2008.pdf.

7. Skramstad, "An Agenda," 123.

8. Your team might be made up of the chair or members of your facilities committee, an architect, a structural engineer, a historian, a contractor (who would not want to bid on future projects), a city/county government representative, a member of your local area's historic preservation group, a lawyer with ADA knowledge, and a risk management assessor. Some of these team members may need to be paid for their services and others may donate their time and expertise.

9. Eleanor Cunningham, e-mail, March 25, 2011.

10. Marjorie Fechtig, e-mail, March 18, 2011.

11. Barbara Ward, e-mail, March 17, 2011.

12. Digital formats are convenient, but technologies change quickly and become obsolete. It is always wise to store hard copies of your records in a secure place for future reference.

13. See "II. National Register Criteria for Evaluation," National Park Service, www .nps.gov/history/nr/publications/bulletins/nrb15/nrb15_2.htm, and "IX. Summary of the National Historic Landmarks Criteria for Evaluation," National Park Service, www .nps.gov/history/nr/publications/bulletins/nrb15/nrb15_9.htm.

14. Heather Quiroga, e-mail, March 18, 2011; Andrea Malcomb, phone conversation, March 25, 2011; "Owner's Manual for Historically Designated Homes & Buildings," Historic Denver, www.historicdenver.org/uploaded-files/Brochure_Final%20 Draft.pdf.

COLLECTIONS MANAGEMENT: KNOW WHAT YOU HAVE, KNOW WHY YOU HAVE IT, KNOW WHERE YOU GOT IT, KNOW WHERE IT IS

Patricia L. Miller

Collections are what set many museums apart from other nonprofit organizations. Intellectual control is at the core of managing those collections. This means that for every object in a museum's collections, the following questions must be answered:

- What is it?
- Why does the museum have it?
- Does the museum own it?
- Where did the museum get it?
- When was it acquired?
- Where is it?
- What condition is it in?

The organization's purpose and mission are the starting points for collecting. A museum's mission statement often defines the scope of collections, identifying the themes, subjects, and types of objects the museum will collect. This tool will aid staff members in deciding if something should be acquired for a collection. The scope may be laid out in the collection policy or, in expanded form, in a collections plan. By defining the collections scope, a museum establishes parameters for collecting that will help it to fulfill its mission. A collections plan goes further by identifying specific collecting goals, how they will be achieved, who will implement them, when the collecting will happen, and what it will cost.[1]

But who decides if objects are appropriate for the museum's collection, and what is the procedure for acquiring title to them? Many museums have a collections or acquisitions committee that evaluates proposed gifts or purchases. Although small museums most commonly acquire collections items through donation, a museum with a well-defined scope and collecting plan may identify significant artifacts to acquire by purchase. No matter the size of a museum, a collections committee helps to make an informed decision about whether an object fits the museum's collections scope and the museum can care for it. The committee documents the reasons for its decision, sometimes using a form to do so (see textbox 3.1). Therefore, the decision to acquire or not is based on an established policy supporting the museum's mission, not on the whim of one person. Maintaining this standard is also helpful when the committee must decline items unrelated to the mission. The recommendation of the collections committee is often ratified by a vote of the museum's board of trustees, which represents the legal face of the museum.

Although museums acquire items for permanent collections with the intent of keeping them, some circumstances require a museum to deaccession (formally remove from the permanent collection) artifacts, which entails a process similar to that for accessioning (formally adding to the permanent collection). The collections committee recommends action to the board, the board ratifies it, and the committee oversees the deaccession. Reasons for deaccessioning should be listed in the collections policy. They might include the deteriorated condition of an object, a documented hazard presented by an item, a duplication of objects within the collection, and the emergence of new information about the object's authenticity. The deaccessioning process should be at least as stringent as the process for acquisition.

Deaccessioning is a sensitive issue and should be approached carefully. Some museums keep it quiet to avoid creating an impression that the institution is selling off its collections. But that can backfire if the deaccessioning becomes public. Other museums take the opportunity to explain the decision and its rationale, feeling that transparency is preferable and the decision is justified. Methods of disposal should be mentioned in the collections policy and can include gift to or trade with another museum or nonprofit, public sale, transfer to the museum's education collection, or witnessed destruction of the object.

Currently, it is recommended that funds realized from the sale of deaccessioned materials be used for the acquisition of new items or the direct care of current collections; however, the latter use is under review in the museum community. Many museums do not capitalize collections (assign a monetary value to them). However, the Federal Accounting Standards Board restricts the use of funds from deaccessioning to the purchase of new collections, unless the collections are capitalized and treated as financial assets. The American Association for State and Local History's statement on capitalizing assets can be accessed online at www.aaslh.org/ethics.htm.

Returning collections artifacts to the original owners is frowned upon, especially if the donors might have taken a tax deduction for the gift. Even if this is not the case, once the property has been legally transferred to the museum, it is held in trust for all the public. Thus, the donor has the same status as the rest of the public.

Maintaining Intellectual Control

While there is no single way to maintain intellectual control over collections, there are standardized procedures for acquiring items, assigning numbers to them, marking objects, and cataloging them. The procedures implement the collection policy. They should be put in writing and reviewed and updated on a regular basis, preferably every three to five years. A good time to review the procedures is when the collections policy is being reviewed.

Photo 3.1. Gloves are often worn when handling museum objects. The primary considerations are whether the objects would be better protected with the gloves on or off, and whether the items themselves might pose a health hazard to the worker. Gloves should always be worn when handling metal objects and photographs.

White cotton gloves and nitrile gloves are the most common types. Latex is another kind, but some people are allergic to them. Gloves with powder coatings should not be worn because the powder might get on the artifacts. Cotton gloves come in various thicknesses and sizes. They should not be worn with anything slippery, such as glass or ceramics. Ones with rubberized dots on the fingers are not recommended, as they can mark some objects. Cotton gloves should be changed frequently. They can be washed and worn again. Disposable nitrile gloves also may be purchased in different sizes. If gloves are not worn, hands should be washed very frequently, not only because of the accumulation of dirt but also because the natural oils in one's hands can harm the artifacts. The oils in some people's hands are highly acidic. No lotion should be worn when handling collections objects. (Courtesy of Illinois Heritage Association)

Several good resources, both printed and online, offer direction for collections management. Daniel Reibel's *Registration Methods for the Small Museum* is especially useful. It contains several practical sections titled "What Not to Do, and When Not to Do It."[2] Generally, the stewardship of a museum's collections is guided by two principles: Do no harm, and make everything reversible. The first principle applies when handling and caring for artifacts. Museum staff members are expected to handle collections far more carefully than would be expected with one's own items. Scrupulously keeping hands clean and wearing gloves are standard practices aimed at preserving items for hundreds of years instead of a generation or two. Artifacts are expected to reflect their history. One wants to be careful about returning them to an earlier condition. Accumulated dirt may be considered historic, and removing it may harm the artifact by altering its authenticity. For the same reason, spray-painting hospital equipment to make it look pristine for an exhibit would not be a recommended practice. Any treatment that alters condition should be undertaken by a trained conservator. The second principle—reversibility—comes into play in applying accession numbers to artifacts. Irreversibly applying numbers (for example, engraving them on glassware or writing with a pen on photographs) harms the artifact by making a permanent change. One also wants to be able to remove the numbers (if, for instance, there is an error in application) without causing damage.

Manual versus Computerized Records

While some museums rely on manual record-keeping systems, more and more institutions are turning to computerized systems to manage their collections. Whatever method is chosen, backup copies of records should be maintained off-site. Several basic kinds of records must be kept on collections. These include accession records, source files (often donor files but possibly purchase records as well), location files, and subject files (or catalog files). With a manual system, records are often kept in notebooks and card files, with perhaps one devoted to each of the topics listed above. The subject files are sometimes meager, even nonexistent, because of the large investment of time in laboriously entering detailed information by hand. Getting to the relevant topical information in a card file may be a cumbersome process requiring sorting through numerous cards to make connections. By contrast, a computerized system allows a worker to use software to enter data into templates or fields, and accession files, source files, location files, and subject files can be integrated. It is far easier to cross-reference information when keeping computerized records. Computers allow many records to be consolidated and card files to be eliminated.

Some museums have not considered it necessary to computerize their records. The manual system works well enough and may have been in place for a long time. People are familiar with it, and it is easy to explain to a new worker or volunteer. However, due to the large amount of time required to enter information by hand and the number of different files that must be separately maintained, the continuation of a manual system has two unfortunate consequences. First, the time invested is drained from other museum needs. Staff or volunteers who spend many hours on card files and indexes cannot perform other needed tasks, and time is a valuable commodity. Second, there is a tendency to delay entering data, which creates a backlog, or even to eliminate some of the records. This problem may not be recognized for some time, but it will eventually cause headaches for those responsible for the collections.

Computerizing records is within the reach of most museums, even very small ones. First, the museum needs an appropriate computer. Second, it must have collections management software. Third, it should be able to gain Internet access in order for staff and volunteers to find up-to-date information that will facilitate collections management. Fourth, selecting a computerized system means making a commitment to upgrade equipment as technology changes.

Before investing in a computer, the museum staff should do a little research and talk to others who have one. The main decision will be whether to go with a PC (a personal computer commonly using Windows) or a Mac (Apple's Macintosh). Another consideration might be whether to get a desktop or a laptop computer. The portability of a laptop makes it convenient to take the computer to the collections for data entry. For lengthy computer work, however, a desktop will be more comfortable for the user. Also, a computer will likely be used in the museum by several people and for numerous tasks, not just collections management. So, again, the desktop might be a more practical choice. Most computers today will probably have enough capacity to handle current collections management software. Internet access will take some study and may be affected by an institution's telephone service. The museum's geographic location will dictate the service that is available.

In addition to bringing together the various kinds of records needed for collections management, data management software can help with more specific tasks. Some museums adapt existing programs and build an in-house system that works for its own collections data. Microsoft Access and FileMaker Pro are two choices. There are programs designed especially for museum collections that can do much more, correlating and cross-referencing information and generating forms, letters, and reports tailored to fit the museum's needs. Some programs are coordinated with the museum's membership records and can be used for fundraising. Some programs include the capacity to integrate digital images of collection objects into the records. There are granting sources that can help purchase this kind of equipment.

Consulting an excellent 2010 master's thesis that reviewed several collections management programs could help determine which is the best choice for a particular situation. The author begins with a fascinating history of the use of computers in museums for collections management.[3] She reviews each of the programs she surveyed (PastPerfect, TMS, EmbARK, Argus, Re:discovery, Vernon CMS, and KE EMu) and includes charts for each with client types and costs. PastPerfect and EmbARK are the cheapest, but EmbARK is used more for art museums and PastPerfect for history museums. PastPerfect is only available for Windows operating systems. She concludes that of the programs studied, EMu appears better equipped to handle large exhibitions than PastPerfect or Re:discovery but is less user-friendly.[4] The thesis appendices include the author's original questionnaire, hardware requirements for the programs, a feature matrix that displays the strong and weak points of each software program, and the complete survey results. Hopefully, this study will be published, but it is currently available from the author by request.[5]

Registration

Someone in the museum must be responsible for overseeing registration procedures. In an institution with a paid staff, this would be a registrar, collections manager, curator, or director; in a large museum, perhaps this would be the conservator. These terms are defined in *Museum Registration Methods*, 5th edition.[6] However, their meanings may vary from museum to museum. In a museum operated solely by volunteers, this responsibility still exists and is often undertaken by a volunteer who manages the collections. The board maintains oversight of the procedures, but someone must keep abreast of current standards and legal and ethical requirements. The registrar is usually the person who keeps the board informed and in compliance. Consolidating collections procedures in a written format that implements the museum's collection policy will help to provide continuity when there is a change in staff. Museums sometimes get into trouble when there is little written documentation about procedures; over time, people forget the procedures or move on, and the system breaks down.

The registration system is the primary means by which the museum maintains intellectual control of the collections. Registration has four key elements: ownership, identification, documentation, and accountability.

Ownership

The museum must acquire clear legal title to the object and any associated rights. Three elements constitute transfer of ownership: an offer, an acceptance, and the physical transfer of the property. This is often accomplished by a deed of gift, sometimes referred to as a DOG. Samples of such a form can be found online and in publications cited in this chapter. Marie Malaro, in her seminal *A Legal Primer on Managing Museum Collections*, provides an excellent form, which includes wording about copyright and associated rights. Such rights exist separately, and unless ownership of them is also transferred, they will not belong to the museum.[7]

The absence of a deed of gift does not mean that the museum has not acquired title. There may be board minutes, inventories, correspondence, copies of receipts, articles in museum newsletters or in newspapers, photos from an exhibit, collection records such as an accessions ledger, or accession numbers on the object. The combination of these elements may constitute proof of an offer, an acceptance, and the transfer of the property.

It is extremely important for a museum to have ownership of the objects in its care. Otherwise, it is expending its time and resources on objects that belong to someone else. (This will be discussed below under "Loans.") Almost every museum has some objects in its collection for which it cannot demonstrate ownership. Some items just seem to appear without any kind of documentation or paper trail. These are often referred to in records as "found in collection" (FIC). Other artifacts have incomplete collections records. What should a museum do about these orphan objects? Many states now have legislation to acquire title to such items. These objects are typically classified as abandoned property. The process of acquiring title is usually long (often taking several years) and requires several actions on the part of the museum, but it is a way of putting the artifacts right with the law.

In some cases, the museum knows the donor and has just never gotten a signed deed of gift. If there is other evidence to support transfer of title (correspondence from the donor, a copy of a receipt from the museum, board minutes), the museum may have enough documentation to demonstrate ownership. This can be important because heirs of a donor sometimes make claim to artifacts, stating that the items were intended as loans, not gifts. This can make for bad press, bad feelings, and bad collections management, because once items have been legally given, the donors have no more right to them than do any other members of the public. The museum holds its collections in trust for all the public. The distinction between a loan and a gift is an important one.

If there is insufficient documentation to verify ownership of certain objects, the museum might consider "confirming" these gifts if the donors are still available. This involves asking the donor to sign a statement confirming that, at a certain time, he or she gave a certain item to the museum. The language can follow that of the current deed of gift form.[8]

Sometimes objects are just dropped off at a museum, possibly at the front desk, or even left on the doorstep. They may be left for identification, donation, or other assorted purposes. In the best case, they will be left with someone who can ask the owner to complete a temporary custody form. This form defines the conditions under which the object is being left, including whether the museum will insure it, the standard of care that will be given, and the duration of temporary custody.[9] If the drop-off is for a donation, the items can be presented to the collections committee, and the acquisition process or return of the items can proceed from there.

An issue in acquiring some collections items is the need for an appraisal. If a donor declares a gift is worth $500 or more, he or she must file a Form 8283 with the Internal Revenue Service (IRS). While both the declaration of value and the filing of the form are the donor's responsibility, some museums provide the donor with the form as a convenience. Gifts worth large amounts of money ($5,000 or more) require an appraisal in order for the donors to take a tax deduction for the gift. The museum must remain hands-off with the appraisal, as the IRS sees the institution as an interested party. The museum cannot perform or pay for the appraisal; if asked to recommend appraisers, the museum should be careful to provide several names. There are regulations about providing the donor with a receipt, documenting when title is transferred (especially important at the end of the year), and clarifying whether the museum is accepting a gift for its permanent collection or for some other purpose, such as an auction. As mentioned earlier, keeping abreast of these regulations is the responsibility of the registrar, but the board needs to maintain oversight.

Identification

Numbering. Each object in a museum's collections should have its own unique identification. While there are many numbering systems (even simply starting at one and going forward), the most common system uses a tripart number comprising the year of acquisition, the number of the acquisition by the museum within that year, and the number assigned to the individual object (e.g., 2010.45.1). Sometimes referred to as trinominal, this is a simple system, but there are a few complications to it.

The first part of the number is easy to understand. At one time, many museums physically marked only the last two or three digits of the year of acquisition on the object, as most collections were acquired sometime during the twentieth century; as the millennium approached, however, more museums began writing out the entire year, and that is usually the custom now.

The middle part of the tripart number gives some people trouble. It must meet two criteria: the same time (of acquisition) and the same source. It is easy to confuse the number of an acquisition within a year and the source of the acquisition, which is most frequently a donor. The first gift from a donor in a particular year would meet the criteria of same time, same source. The system goes off track when the museum keeps associating that same middle number with future gifts by that same donor, and the original middle number essentially becomes a donor number, even getting repeated in future years. For example, a gift from Mrs. Jones in the year 2010 could have the middle number "45," indicating that it is the forty-fifth acquisition by the museum for 2010. This number might represent one item or many items. The gift from Mrs. Jones might be one dish or a complete set of china, several quilts, five umbrellas, and a dozen pairs of gloves. All would get the middle number "45." But if Mrs. Jones returns with a new gift later that year or in another year, the middle part of the accession number would not be "45." That gift would not meet the criteria of same time, same source.

The last part of the tripart accession number refers to the object. Here complications can arise if objects have several pieces or parts or if items come in sets. A little reading about standard practices can be helpful here—for example, learning when to add an extension to the third number.[10] A set of dishes may be assigned the object number "12," but the individual dishes in the set receive a suffix, making their numbers "12.1," "12.2," and so on. A third number in the tripart accession number assigned to a pair of gloves might be "7," but each glove in the pair receives that number with an *a* or *b* appended, as "7a" and "7b." The most important thing, however, is to be consistent. Once a museum has determined its way of assigning object numbers, it should put the procedure in writing and stick with it, because not every museum does it the same way.

There are a few other considerations about numbering objects. A well-meaning but unfortunate practice that some museums fall into is prefacing an accession number with a letter representing a category, such as *T* for "tools." This introduces a new concept, linking the subject matter of the object to its accession number. The purpose of the accession number is to provide tracking and identification. Imposing a letter that attempts to classify the objects by subject only creates confusion. *M* for "military" (or was that "manufacturing"?) just muddies the water. In many cases, the relationship of the letter to its meaning becomes lost over time.

There are other reasons why some museums preface a number with a letter. They may wish to identify a totally different type of collection. In addition to maintaining the permanent collection, museums often place reproductions or low-quality objects in an education or study collection. These objects might be used in educational programs and handled by visitors (i.e., consumptive use, as described in chapter 1 of this book). Such collections are not held to the high standard of care to which the permanent collection must adhere. Objects used for educational purposes might have an *E* appended to them and be numbered and stored separately from the permanent collection. Such items would not be accessioned but would have their own tripart numbering system.

Museums may also wish to keep track of office equipment and props used in exhibits. These items might be given inventory numbers, using a three-part number preceded by an *I*. This system would help a museum track depreciation of certain kinds of equipment. These items, however, are properties, not collections, and should not be confused with them. They should not be accessioned.

Another use of letters might be to identify collections associated with particular buildings in a site (such as *L* for "log cabin," or *C* for "courthouse"). This would be a way to keep these collections separate from each other. A limited number of collections would be distinguished by the letters, whereas the combinations of letters that might be used to create subject categories could be quite extensive. The latter system would only confuse people and would not comply with the rationale for using accession numbers: to identify and track an artifact. Other ways to classify artifacts are preferable, as is discussed below.

Accession numbers may be assigned once an object has been accepted by the museum into its permanent collection. Some museums wait to assign a number and actually put it on the artifact until after the donor signs the deed of gift and returns it to the museum, thereby completing the transfer of title. A useful way to track accession and inventory numbers is to use a corresponding written log, perhaps kept in a three-ring notebook, with sections for the types of collections. Numbers could be entered manually or could be listed on printouts from the computer. With the ubiquity of computers, some museums no longer use logbooks. The accession information in the logbook is generally transferred to a bound ledger that becomes a permanent record, called the accessions ledger. Many museums with computerized records still retain the bound accessions ledger. Essential accession information (number, source, date, brief description) is entered in ink on numbered pages. The ledger cannot be altered and thus can serve as a legal record if needed. This cannot be said of computerized records. Information from the ledger should be periodically copied and stored off-site.

Accessioning. Once the legal transfer of title that completes an acquisition is finalized, the next step is to complete an accession form and enter the information in the records. Some museums enter information manually on a paper record that includes brief information about all the artifacts in the accession: object names, accession numbers, source, method of acquisition, date received, and date accessioned. This starts the initial accession record for the items in an accession. This information can be transferred to an accession record in a computer.

Documentation

Information about an item's association with people, places, or events should be recorded. The object's historical context—its provenance—is an important part of its identity. The best time to get essential information about the life history of an artifact is when it comes into the museum. Some museums gather information about proposed acquisitions that will conform to their mission. Here is an opportunity to explore how the object fits the museum's scope

TEXTBOX 3.1

THE "WHY KEEP IT?" SHEET

Date:

Reviewer:

Mission:

Brief description of object:

Justification for acquisition (how object fulfills purpose/mission):

Would the object be appropriate for

__exhibition __programs __research

Describe use:

If rejected for acquisition, why?

__not within mission/collecting scope

__poor condition

__too difficult to store or preserve

__duplicate

__other (describe)

Source: Adapted from the Museum Association of Douglas County, Illinois.

of collections and whether it will help the museum tell a particular story.[11] The chance to talk to the donor or to link objects and their stories may bring important insights. Details unavailable or overlooked when an artifact comes to the museum may be lost forever.

Information can also be gleaned from a single object or a group of related objects. In one museum, a nondescript checked shirt from the Depression era took on new significance when it was noticed that many hours had been spent making a precisely aligned patch on one of its elbows, giving it new life. A girl's graduation dress and matching shoes were enhanced by a photograph, given with the dress, of the graduate wearing the dress and holding her diploma. The diploma filed elsewhere without a note might have lost its association with the other artifacts.

Cataloging. Completing catalog work sheets is an essential step, although documentation is an ongoing process, and new research may add to the record. The work sheets can be tailored to fit the collection and even the types of items within it, such as photographs, objects, or library items. The sheets contain fields on which information can be entered for each object, such as object name, accession number, source, method of acquisition, dates, value, maker, condition, location, description, measurements, provenance (history), and usually the initials of the person completing the work sheet and the date the entry was made. The museum can generate its own work sheet format, but if it has collections management software, forms can usually be printed out on which a worker enters the information by hand in the same order in which it will ultimately be entered into the computer. Although printed work sheets are usually filled in by hand, some museum workers enter data about the artifact directly into the computer, bypassing manual entry on the work sheets. Others find this actually slows the process, especially if one is wearing gloves while handling objects or trying to take measurements. Some museums divide the tasks, having one person manually enter the information on the work sheets and another person enter the data into the computer once several work sheets have accumulated. In other institutions, workers enter the catalog work sheet data at the same time that they complete the accession work sheets. In still other cases, a worker may be transferring previously compiled records into a computerized system without needing to have the objects at hand. There are many different ways to complete the catalog records. Museums need to tailor the process to fit their individual situations. Completed work sheets, whether generated by hand or by computer, should be retained. Having a paper backup for records often turns out to be very helpful.

Before beginning the use of work sheets, and in order to maintain consistency, one should spend some time thinking about the various pieces of information that will be entered on the sheet (such as dates, condition, and measurements). Dates, for instance, may be entered in a number of ways, and the work sheet may contain more than one field for dates. There are range dates (1900–1920), circa dates (c. 1865), the date something was made, and dates of use. If using a computer, one also has to think about how the information will be sorted or retrieved. For instance, a circa date (c. 1865) would be sorted by "c." For some programs, one would invert the order to "1865 c." In addition, there are conventions regarding the description of condition that can provide consistency, including using standard terminology for condition reporting.[12] At one time, when measuring objects, everyone began switching to the metric system, but using inches now is often the norm. Some museums include both. Some software programs allow for choices in terminology for measurements. Description and provenance are work sheet fields that encourage a narrative. Some practice in communicating this information can help the worker to be precise and succinct, avoiding repetition of information given in other fields.

Marking. Accession numbers should be physically applied to the artifacts where possible. Some standard methods are used to apply the numbers. The materials used for marking and the ways they are applied are different for different types of artifacts. The materials and methods should not harm the object and should be reversible. For example, nonadhesive cloth tape on which accession numbers have been applied with ink can be sewn onto clothing and textiles. Cotton twill or linen tape available from archival supply houses is recommended. Certain kinds of ink pens are preferred because the ink will not run or fade. Alternatively, typed labels sewn with Tyvek or Reemay can be used. There are techniques to sew the label on by inserting the needle in the weave so as not to break any threads in the original artifact, and knots should not be used. Positioning of the labels should be consistent.[13]

A common technique for three-dimensional objects is to apply numbers directly on the artifact with pens over a clear barrier coat. The barrier coat needs to be removable without harming the artifact. Some materials used in labeling are toxic and should be used with appropriate care and ventilation. Clear fingernail polish was used for many years as a barrier coat, but it is no longer considered acceptable because it sometimes flakes off or turns yellow over time. In addition, the core ingredient of fingernail polish, cellulose nitrate, is an unstable material. A top barrier coat of the proper material is applied over the accession number to create a layered number application that can be removed if needed. A number might have to be removed for any number of reasons, including an error in marking; a change in technology, including new information about harm caused by the materials (as happened with nail polish) or new methods such as microchips; a transfer from the permanent collection to an education collection; or a possible eradication due to the deaccessioning of an object.

TEXTBOX 3.2

UNACCEPTABLE MARKING METHODS AND MATERIALS

This list is modified from one presented in Tamara Johnston and Robin Meador-Woodruff, "Marking," in *Museum Registration Methods*, ed. Rebecca A. Buck and Jean Allman Gilmore, 5th edition (Washington, DC: American Association of Museums Press, 2010), 247–48 (reprinted with permission). The marking chapter includes extensive charts that detail preferred methods and materials for applying numbers to many types of objects. For more information, visit www.aam-us.org/bookstore.

The following materials should *not* be used:

- *Pressure-sensitive tape (including cellophane, masking, adhesive, and embossing tapes):* The adhesive on some of these tapes sticks more and more tightly to the object as time passes and may become difficult to remove without strong solvents. Other tapes dry out and fall off, leaving behind a sticky residue or stain.
- *Pressure-sensitive labels:* The adhesive on many pressure-sensitive (self-stick) labels can deteriorate within several months to a sticky residue that penetrates paper products. The labels also have a tendency to fall off over time as the solvent in the adhesive evaporates.
- *Gummed (water-moistened) paper labels:* The adhesives on these labels can stain and are difficult to remove from some materials. On other materials they have poor adhesive quality and are not durable.
- *Rubber cement:* This adhesive behaves somewhat like pressure-sensitive labels and should be avoided. It can stain organic materials and tarnish metals.
- *Silicone products:* Silicones are generally nonreversible, and other marking materials will not adhere well to them.
- *Spray varnishes:* It is difficult to control where the spray will land. In addition, some materials may yellow and become brittle or difficult to remove.
- *Typewriter correction fluid:* This material has been used as a white base coat on dark objects. Many correction fluids have poor durability and tend to dry out and flake as they age. Others may prove solvent resistant with age.
- *Nail polish:* The exact formula and aging properties of these polishes cannot be determined. Some polishes will peel with age, taking the accession number and part of the surface of the object with them.

- *Nail-polish remover:* Commercial nail-polish remover may contain additives such as perfume, oil, dye, and gelatin, in addition to the solvent.
- *Ballpoint ink:* Most ballpoint inks tend to smear and can become difficult to remove with age. Many are not lightfast. Some contain iron gall, which is very acidic and corrosive.
- *Permanent marker:* Most permanent markers are not lightfast, will bleed easily, and are acidic.
- *Chalks:* These materials are not durable. They smear indefinitely and can be difficult to remove from porous materials without strong solvents.
- *Fusible iron-on fabrics:* These materials should not be used for labeling textiles. The adhesives leave a residue and may damage textiles.
- *Metal-edged tags:* The metal can corrode and stain objects.
- *Wire:* Wires can corrode or abrade objects and may tear fragile or soft surfaces.
- *Nails, pins, staples, screws, and other metal fasteners:* Metals may corrode and stain objects, cause corrosion of metal objects that they are in contact with, leave permanent holes, or cause splitting or cracking of woods and other materials.

Paper items and photographs should have numbers written on them with special pencils. The numbers should be removable, and their placement should be considered. In photographs, for instance, one wants to avoid writing on the back of the image when possible. Unfortunately, photos often arrive in museum collections with information scrawled on their backs, which can eventually obliterate the image as the ink bleeds through. Pressure from pens sometimes transfers the writing to the image surface. Ballpoint pens are particularly bad culprits.

Applying numbers to some artifacts is not advised or may not be possible due to the object's size, fragility, or material. In such cases, archival cardboard tags are usually tied on with string, or tags are placed near the artifacts, possibly in a box or sleeve. The potential problem with this method is that the tag can become separated from the artifact, especially if the artifact is moved or put on exhibit. Good photo documentation of the artifact can help avoid this problem, and some collections software programs now have a digitization component built in. Still, the use of tags is not as reliable as placing a number on the object. More considerations relate to types of objects and how to mark them properly. Several good sources of instruction on applying numbers are available inexpensively in printed form as well as online.[14] This is also a popular topic for short courses and workshops.

Classification. Classification systems exist to help museums catalog their artifacts in order to maintain their documentation. Art museums use the Art and Architecture Thesaurus. History museums use the Nomenclature for Museum Cataloging, a system devised by Robert G. Chenhall that identifies ten categories of objects by how they were made or used. Most artifacts can be classified using this hierarchy.[15] Information about classification is typically put in subject (or catalog) files. Some collections software incorporates the nomenclature classification system, and artifacts are automatically entered into the correct category. The nomenclature classification system could be utilized in a manual system using index cards.

Having subject files is very useful on several fronts. When items are offered to the museum, one can verify whether they will be duplicates, add to existing themes, or fill a gap. Subject files are valuable in exploring ideas for exhibitions and programs. They are also repositories for ongoing research by both museum staff members and visiting scholars, which can shed new light on the meaning of the collection items.

Accountability

Access. The museum has a responsibility to make information about the collections available to the public. Accession files typically contain correspondence regarding the accession, along with corroborating information about provenance, exhibit and loan history, insurance records, reports about repairs or conservation, and notes on changes in condition. Some information may need to be restricted due to privacy concerns and other considerations, such as value. Decisions about access may be made by the collections committee based on the collections policy, but the procedures for enforcing will then be the responsibility of the registrar or collections manager.

Location. The museum must establish a system for locating the objects in its collections. A different system will work with different types of museums. For a house museum where certain things are on exhibit in one location for extended periods, a system that correlates the object with its historical period may be most efficient. Thus, most objects live in a certain place, and if they are moved, the move will be recorded. Something quite different will be needed for a museum with multiple sites where things are often moved from place to place or for a museum that holds frequent temporary exhibits or loans things from its collections to other museums. If artifacts are shifted about, it is crucial to track their movements. It is folly to think one can just remember where they went. Without good records, tracking location will become a nightmare. A museum should easily and quickly be able to use its records to locate any object and, conversely, to locate the records associated with any object. The accession number is usually the key to tracking the location of the artifact. This is one area in which a computerized system will facilitate record keeping.

Storage. Accountability requires organized and protected storage environments. Incoming items can be isolated so that they can be checked for infestations. A processing area where new acquisitions can be worked on should be set aside. Organized storage areas with numbered units and shelves will help workers to locate specific items. A museum must not only know where the objects are but also take responsibility for monitoring their condition. Some museums put almost everything on exhibit and allocate very little space to storage. This shortens the life of the artifacts by exposing them to light and dust. It also decreases opportunities for visitors to return to see something new and tends to mean that many more items are crammed into an exhibit than can clearly tell the intended story. The level of care shown to objects not being exhibited is just as important as that given to those on display.

Small museums often have limited funds to spend on storage and limited space to allocate to it. But storage should be recognized as a stewardship priority. Responsible museums include some amount for storage and collections care in their budgets. Collections storage should be isolated from other museum functions. A long-standing formula recommended for space allocation is 40:40:20—40 percent for storage and related processing, 40 percent for exhibits, and 20 percent for administrative and other uses.[16] In a museum that may not be able to control environmental conditions, it is especially important that the collections be kept in areas where light and dust are minimized; fluctuations in the environment can be controlled by creating barrier layers (such as packing objects in archival materials and placing them in boxes), thereby minimizing the effects of spikes in temperature and humidity.

Inventorying. Museums need to know what they have and where the items are. Without conducting an inventory, this cannot be verified. Museums may conduct spot inventories that target a selected number of artifacts and their records. This is helpful but limited in scope. Periodically, perhaps on a rotating basis covering three to five years, the entire collection needs to be inventoried. The process will identify missing items or any gaps in records, and it will uncover any problems in condition. Such discoveries could lead to better collection-related planning, possibly supported by a grant to improve storage conditions. Once a problem is recognized, steps can be taken to rectify it.

The inventory process may proceed from an examination of records, comparing them to actual objects, it may start with the objects and proceed to locating their records, or it may encompass both methods. An inventory is most efficiently accomplished by two people working in tandem or by inventory teams. Before beginning, everyone involved in the inventory should review procedures for handling artifacts. Creating a form containing fields for information will allow workers to enter coded answers and save time in the inventory process. It is important to be thorough and to identify all components of artifacts with multiple parts. The inventory process will very likely uncover undocumented or FIC artifacts. Invariably, the inventory also will reveal that some objects are missing. There may be backlogged artifacts that have not yet been accessioned, items that are on loan to the museum, or records of items that have been loaned out by the museum. All of these situations should be anticipated and responses planned. Having a process in place to note what is needed and flagging the records for later action will keep the process from bogging down. This is another situation where computerized data can be helpful.

Risk management. The registrar is the most likely person to have responsibility for safeguarding the collections. This includes controlling access to them and to their records, having oversight of the environment for the collections, and planning for emergencies and disasters. Security for collections, both on exhibit and in storage, is a special concern for small museums because funds for equipment are limited, and responsibilities overlap among staff and volunteers. Often, many people have access to both the collections and their records. Storage areas should be locked and some records isolated for confidentiality, but it can be difficult to adhere to these practices. Some people who work with collections come to feel personal ownership of them. This is another instance in which having written procedures backed up by a strong collections policy and a code of ethics can be invaluable. Still, someone has to be the enforcer, with the support of the governing body. Often the registrar, more than anyone else, has the responsibility to maintain oversight and enforce collections standards. The registrar is the gatekeeper who sees that policies and procedures are adhered to and that there is no personal use of collections or any personal benefit to an individual from association with them.

The registrar or collections manager also has the most day-to-day contact with the collections and knows how environmental conditions may be affecting them. This person can offer guidance on mitigating environmental risks and addressing potential hazards in the face of disasters and is a key player in developing a disaster plan. The registrar is usually responsible for any issues relating to insurance of the collections. Although many small museums do not insure collections, believing that the artifacts are unique and irreplaceable, some museums have found that in the event of a complete disaster, having funds to rebuild collections may be helpful, and if there is damage to collections, funds for their conservation may also make a difference in the future of the museum. (See chapter 1 of Book 3 in this series for more discussion about insuring collections.)

Legal and ethical concerns. Numerous laws affect museums of all sizes and types. Small museums are not immune from accountability requirements, and they may be affected in ways not immediately obvious. Provisions of the Native American Graves Protection and Repatriation Act, for instance, apply to any museum that receives federal funds. This legislation regulates the ownership and disposition of human remains, funerary objects, sacred objects, and objects of cultural patrimony of Native Americans and their lineal descendents. A museum not directly supported by federal funds might think it is not covered by this law, but it could receive local or state funds (perhaps through a grant) originating at the federal level and thus be subject to the regulations. Museums are also covered by federal wildlife and endangered species laws. As places of public accommodation, museums are covered by the Americans with Disabilities Act. Someone in the museum needs to take responsibility for being aware of how these and other legal requirements may affect the institution, and that person may be the registrar. Chapter 4 in Book 2 in this series provides more detail on legal issues.

The museum should support training for the registrar to enable him or her to keep up to date on legal and ethical issues that affect museums.

Loans

Borrowing objects can enhance a museum's ability to tell many stories. Artifacts may be borrowed from individuals, other museums, or even for-profit entities. Guidelines can help a museum navigate some of the legal and ethical concerns that may arise in seeking or making loans.[17] The museum's collection policy and code of ethics can also give direction. The collections manager will probably be the individual entrusted with the details of the arrangements. For example, all incoming and outgoing loans should be accompanied by condition reports. Loan forms are typically generated by the lending museum, but they can be issued by the borrower. Sample forms can be found in numerous publications.[18] Long-term, or "permanent," loans are frowned upon, and most museums today borrow only for short, defined periods (perhaps a year or less) with the opportunity for renewal. But there are exceptions. In some cases, as when a museum borrows from a governmental entity or a university, long-term loans are unavoidable. However, such loans mean that a museum is incurring costs for items it does not own, which is generally a poor fiscal practice.

As mentioned above, it is especially important when dealing with individual donors to make sure both parties are clear about whether an item is intended as a loan or a gift. A deed of gift and other written documents can provide a solid framework for later reference. This is an area in which some museums have encountered problems over time. When museums are just starting, it is common for community members to bring in their belongings. Everyone wants to pitch in and help, and formalities such as deeds of gift or receipts are often overlooked. As time passes and donors move away or die, the status of the items becomes unclear. An item originally intended as a gift may now be remembered as a loan, or a donor's heirs may see the gift as a loan. Sometimes items can no longer be found or lack accession numbers to distinguish them from other similar objects. Some very unpleasant situations can arise. Since returning gifts where there has been a legal transfer of title is considered a poor practice, whether or not it might be scrutinized by the IRS, it is important for the museum to get it right in the beginning.

Museums often loan items from their own collections. These transactions too will be governed by the collections policy. The registrar or collections manager will be responsible for seeing that the artifacts are protected en route and cared for in a manner that meets the lending museum's own standards. Typically, items from a museum's permanent collection are loaned only to another museum or to a comparable nonprofit organization, not to an individual. Some museums use a standard facility report to determine if a borrowing museum meets accepted standards. The *General Facilities Report* (formerly called the *Standard Facilities Report*) is a detailed form that can be purchased from the Registrars Committee of the American Association of Museums. Most small museums do not go to this extent, but they might gain some ideas to consider by looking at a copy of the standard facility report. Copies may be available to review in statewide museum association libraries or in museums that use them.

A Viable Collections Management System

The basic guidelines for maintaining good collections records are to

- assign responsibilities to a specific person and give that person support from the board;
- align procedures with the collections policy, other relevant policies, and the museum's code of ethics;
- put the procedures in writing;
- review and update the procedures periodically;
- provide the staff with the proper tools and access to information to do the job.

Management of collections happens primarily behind the scenes. Good and bad practices might not be immediately evident, but ultimately a museum's reputation will be linked to how well it manages and cares for the collections it holds in trust for the public. There will come a time when it becomes known whether a museum is meeting accepted standards, and it will be judged accordingly. Consistent efforts to meet these standards will pay off in the long run.

Acknowledgments

Thanks to Carol Betts, Illinois Heritage Association editor, for insightful comments and suggestions; to Ginger Gomez and Jennifer Griffin at PastPerfect Museum Software for information about computerizing museum records; to Elena Carpinone for permission to use material from her thesis on software programs; to the authors, editors, and publisher of *Museum Registration Methods*, 5th edition, for permission to modify the list of unacceptable marking materials and methods; and to Barbara Oehlschlaeger-Garvey at the Early American Museum in Mahomet, Illinois, for a discussion of accessioning practices.

Resources

In addition to sources listed in the notes, short published articles on collections management may be found in the libraries of statewide museum service organizations and state historical societies. Easily accessible resources can be found online. Some useful resources are listed below.

- American Institute for Conservation of Historic and Artistic Works (www .conservation-us.org): This website offers articles about conservation and museum documentation.
- Gerald R. Ford Conservation Center, Nebraska State Historical Society (www .nebraskahistory.org/conserve/treasures/pdfs.htm): These articles concern caring for artifacts and related topics such as handling, cleaning, storage, environmental monitoring, and housing of artifacts.
- National Park Service *Conserve O Grams* (http://www.nps.gov/museum/publications/conserveogram/conserv.html): *Conserve O Grams* are short articles, or leaflets, primarily directed toward care of collections; however, some address marking artifacts, storage considerations, security, and disaster planning.
- *National Park Service Museum Handbook, Part 2: Museum Records* (www.nps.gov/ history/museum/publications/handbook.html): This comprehensive document, the second of three parts, outlines procedures for museum record keeping, including accessioning, cataloging, loans, deaccessioning, photography, and reporting annual collections management data. Part 1 of the handbook is titled *Museum Collections*, and Part 3 is titled *Museum Collections Use*. All three parts of the handbook are also available in printed form.
- Northeast Document Conservation Center Preservation Leaflets (www.nedcc .org/resources/leaflets.list.php): These leaflets are primarily oriented toward the

care of paper-based items, but they sometimes cover management issues. Topics include preservation planning, environmental concerns, emergency management, and storage.

Notes

1. American Association of Museums (AAM). *National Standards and Best Practices for U.S. Museums* (Washington, DC: AAM, 2008), 90.

2. Daniel E. Reibel, *Registration Methods for the Small Museum*, 3rd ed. (Walnut Creek, CA: AltaMira Press, 1997), 42–43, 76, 82, 102–3, 118.

3. Elana C. Carpinone, "Museum Collections Management Systems: One Size Does *NOT* Fit All" (master's thesis, Seaton Hall University, May 2010), 128–29.

4. Carpinone, "Museum Collections Management Systems," 7–22.

5. The author can be reached by e-mail at carpin75@potsdam.edu.

6. Rebecca A. Buck and Jean Allman Gilmore, *Museum Registration Methods*, 5th ed. (Washington, DC: American Association of Museums, 2010), 13.

7. Marie C. Malaro, *A Legal Primer on Managing Museum Collections*, 2nd ed. (Washington, DC: Smithsonian Institution Press, 1998), 209–10.

8. Malaro, *A Legal Primer*, 205.

9. Malaro, *A Legal Primer*, 349–54.

10. Buck and Gillmore, *Museum Registration Methods*, 171.

11. On its website, the Chicago History Museum lists five areas that define the scope of its collecting; see www.chicagohs.org/research/aboutcollection/index#scope (accessed January 4, 2010).

12. Buck and Gilmore, *Museum Registration Methods*, 57–60.

13. Buck and Gilmore, *Museum Registration Methods*, 73–74.

14. See, for example, Marianna James Munyer, "How To . . . Mark Objects in Museum Collections, Part 1: Barrier Coats, Pens, Inks, Paints," *Illinois Association of Museums News* 16 (summer 1997), and "How To . . . Mark Objects in Museum Collections, Part 2: Tags, Direct Marking, and Difficult Materials," *Illinois Association of Museums News* 17 (October 1997). Copies are available for a small fee from the Illinois Association of Museums and can be ordered online at www.state.il.us/HPA/iam/publications.html (accessed January 4, 2010). The Registrars Committee of the American Association of Museums has produced a very informative booklet containing detailed information on how to mark objects and what to use—and not use—for this purpose. It includes information on marking plastics and archeological artifacts and making archival copies of unstable paper records. See *Beyond Fingernail Polish III* (workshop handbook prepared for the annual meeting of the Registrars Committee of the American Association of Museums, Portland, Oregon, May 22, 2003). Also see Buck and Gilmore, *Museum Registration Methods*, 233–75, for details on marking many items. The Minnesota Historical Society has a two-part article available online; see Gina Nicole Delfino, "Recommendations for Applying Accession Numbers to Museum Objects: Part 1," *Tech Talk: Artifact Labeling I* (May 2000), available at www.mnhs.org/about/publications/techtalk/TechTalkMay2000.pdf, and Gina Nicole Delfino, "Recommendations for Ap-

plying Accession Numbers to Museum Objects: Part 2," *Tech Talk: Artifact Labeling II* (July 2000), available at www.mnhs.org/about/publications/techtalk/techtalkjuly2000 .pdf (both accessed January 4, 2010).

15. For the latest, expanded version of Chenhall's system, see Paul Bourcier, Ruby Rogers, and the American Association for State and Local History's Nomenclature Committee, *Nomenclature 3.0 for Museum Cataloging*, 3rd ed. (Blue Ridge Summit, PA: AltaMira Press, 2009).

16. Carl E. Guthe, *The Management of Small History Museums* (Nashville, TN: American Association for State and Local History, 1964), 14.

17. The American Association of Museums (AAM) has issued guidelines for exhibiting borrowed objects, developing and managing business support, and related topics; see "Museum Ethics," AAM, www.aam-us.org/museumresources/ethics/index.cfm (accessed January 4, 2010).

18. Reibel, *Registration Methods*, 174–79; Malaro, *A Legal Primer*, 253–59, 265–73; Buck and Gilmore, *Museum Registration Methods*, 497–98.

DO WE REALLY WANT THAT BUST OF JESUS, AND WHAT SHOULD WE DO WITH THE PUMP ORGAN IN THE OTHER ROOM? OR, WHY YOU WANT A GOOD COLLECTIONS MANAGEMENT POLICY

Julia Clark

As museum people, we all love our collections and know how important they can be to all we do. Because of this, we want to manage and care for our collections in a manner consistent with professional standards, legal requirements, and ethical guidelines. A collections management policy (CMP) is the primary policy document that governs how we bring in, care for, and remove objects from museum collections. According to John Simmons, "The collections management policy ensures that collections are acquired legally and ethically; are appropriate to and advance the museum's mission; and are properly managed, housed, secured, conserved, documented, and used" (2006, 3).

Why Should We Have a Collections Management Policy?

The American Precision Museum (APM) in Windsor, Vermont, holds the largest collection of historically significant machine tools in the nation. It also has many board members who know a lot about precision manufacturing and love to see equipment in action. However, most of them do not have a lot of experience with museum practice. According to collections manager Beau Harris, the APM's CMP is essential to guiding the use and management of the collection in a way that balances preservation and interpretation. The policy clearly distinguishes permanent and programmatic collections so that the APM may best meet its mission.

In Dripping Springs, Texas, the Dr. Pound Historical Farmstead has a pump organ sitting in a storage building on its property. As far as staff members can determine, it has nothing to do with Dr. Pound or the early settlement of Dripping Springs. Unfortunately, they also do not know whom it belongs to, exactly when it showed up, or why the museum has it. Staff would like to find this organ a better home, but it is difficult to remove something from your collection when you are not even sure that you own it. The Dr. Pound Historical Farmstead now has a CMP that clearly defines what it will acquire and how,

CASE STUDY: THE ABBE MUSEUM

The Abbe Museum is now a medium-sized museum, but this has not always been the case. In 1982, when the Abbe adopted its first collections policy, it employed a part-time, seasonal director and one or two seasonal guest services staff. The board president, who was also the chair of the collections committee, was inspired to create the policy through her work with larger museums in New England—she could clearly see the benefits of having such a policy. And in many ways, today's Abbe Museum Collections Management Policy is essentially the same as that first document. As staff changed and grew, changes were made to better define who made decisions and was responsible for implementing the plan. As laws changed—for instance, with the passage of the Native American Graves Protection and Repatriation Act (NAGPRA)—the policy was updated to incorporate their requirements. When controversial acquisition decisions had to be made, the CMP was the guiding document. As the Abbe gained better intellectual control over the collections, the policy allowed the museum, whose mission focuses on the Wabanaki, the native people of Maine, to deaccession a bust of Jesus that had somehow ended up in the collection. Now that the museum has grown to the point where it has added a second facility with a top-notch collections storage area, the CMP continues to guide decisions so as to best manage the collections to meet the mission.

In this chapter you will learn more about what a collections management policy is, why it is important, and how to create one for your organization.

as well as how to properly document new acquisitions, so that the museum will not end up with any more mystery pump organs. Staff can also follow museum policy and Texas law regarding abandoned property to find the owner of the organ or find it a new home.

These are just a couple of examples of really good reasons to have a collections management policy. Ask any of your small museum colleagues who have a CMP, and they will be able to give you many more examples. So, how do you go about creating this very important document for your organization?

Collections Management Policy: Procedure or Plan?

It is important to distinguish between a policy and a procedure. While some basic procedural steps are often included in a CMP, detailed procedures should

CASE STUDY: THE DR. POUND HISTORICAL FARMSTEAD

In 2008, part-time director Marianne Simmons and volunteer Lauren Neugebauer of the Dr. Pound Historical Farmstead in Dripping Springs, Texas, were reviewing the application materials for a grant they hoped to receive. When they came to the list of attachments required, one of the requested documents was a collections management policy. But the Dr. Pound Historical Farmstead did not have a CMP; in fact, Simmons and Neugebauer had never heard of one! So they contacted the Texas Historical Commission (THC), the state agency that provides technical assistance for small history organizations like the farmstead. The staff at the commission provided them with some basic guidelines for creating a CMP and a number of examples from other organizations around Texas. With these resources in hand, Simmons and Neugebauer tackled what seemed at first like a daunting task. In the end, having drawn on about six different sample policies and other resources provided by the THC, they were successful in creating a CMP that would carry their institution forward. The farmstead now has a collections committee and a new director, both guided by the policy and able to follow professional standards and practices with this valuable document in place.

be part of a separate document. Any policies created by a museum must be approved by its governing body (e.g., board of trustees, city council, county commissioners), while procedures can be developed by staff and are meant to guide everyday activities at the museum. Once a procedures manual is created, it is important to keep it up to date and to make sure that any changes to the CMP are reflected in the related procedures.

A good collecting plan is a valuable companion to a collections management policy and helps guide implementation of the acquisitions, accessions, and deaccessions sections of the CMP. (See chapter 5 in this book for more information on collections planning.)

Several excellent resources are available when you decide to tackle writing or revising a collections management policy. The book *Things Great and Small: Collections Management Policies*, by John E. Simmons, was published by the American Association of Museums (AAM) in 2006. Simmons provides background about CMPs and describes each component of a comprehensive plan. For many smaller museums, some of the sections may be combined or may not be necessary. *Things Great and Small* is a key source used in writing this chapter.

Some of the best resources are the collections management policies of other museums. When looking for examples of existing CMPs to help create your own, it may be especially useful to find examples from institutions with similar missions, similar types of collections, and similar forms of governance. Samples are available from the AAM's Information Center (to members), and you will find that other museums in your region are often happy to share their policy documents. However, as you draw on samples and examples from other museum, make sure you do more than just cut and paste. Each organization is unique and needs to make sure it customizes its CMP to its specific needs. Do not include material that does not apply to your museum, and pay special attention to areas that are particularly important or pose special challenges for your collections and mission.

You may also want to refer to standards-of-excellence programs, including the American Association for State and Local History's (AASLH) Standards and Excellence Program for History Organizations and the AAM's Accreditation Program, to identify key subjects to include in your CMP.

Key Sections of a Collections Management Policy

The following is a general summary of some of the key elements of a good CMP. A CMP is really several policies gathered into one document. You may find that some of these sections can be combined or may not be necessary for your museum. Or you may find that additional sections are needed. This is simply a starting point. It is important to note that some parts of a good collections management policy address legal requirements while others address ethical guidelines (textbox 4.3).

Introduction

The introductory section generally includes the museum's mission and vision, a brief history of the museum, and how the museum is governed. This sets the foundation, since a museum's collections should always be appropriate to its mission.

You may include information in the introduction or in a separate section stating who has the authority to make decisions regarding the collections. If your museum has a collections committee, your CMP should describe how the committee is formed, what it is responsible for, and how decisions are made.

Who is responsible for approving new acquisitions and deciding if the museum should accession a particular object or collection? This responsibility may fall to the governing body (i.e., board of trustees), to a collections committee appointed by the governing body, or to a designated staff person. In some cases,

LEGAL AND ETHICAL COMPONENTS OF A CMP

Examples of Legal Requirements
- Clear and legal title for acquisitions
- State laws regarding old loans or abandoned property
- The Native American Graves Protection and Repatriation Act

Examples of Ethical Guidelines
- Acceptable means of disposal of deaccessioned items
- Appropriate use of proceeds from sale of deaccessioned items (although tax law may also create legal requirements)
- Personal collecting guidelines

the responsibility may be divided. For example, some museums allow the director or curator to make decisions on acquisitions offered as donations but require the approval of the collections committee for any purchases. The authority to make such decisions should be clearly defined on your CMP (see textbox 4.4). You may also want to define who signs your deed of gift and to include a current copy of your deed of gift form in the appendices.

Scope and Categories of Collections

The scope of your collections should include a succinct description of the collection. It may include some basic guidelines as to what the museum does or does not collect and how the collection is used.

Categories of the collection should be defined and briefly described. These categories may include the permanent collection, educational or interpretive collection, research collection, and archives. Categories may be based on the type of material in the collection, the level of care or access provided to each category, or both. A museum's permanent collection is generally the core collection, most essential to the mission, and receives the highest level of care. You may also have objects that can be used in exhibits or educational programs, which may not need the same level of care. These are often duplicates, reproductions, or materials that can be easily replaced if damaged or worn out. Archival materials and library collections are often separate categories in order to allow for their differing purposes and to best use and manage these different types of materials and information.

DYER LIBRARY/SACO MUSEUM COLLECTIONS POLICY (EXCERPT)

Role of the Collections Committee
The Collections Committee shall work with the museum, library, and archives staff in the development and review of collections policies, projects, and programs. Day-to-day management of the organization's collections shall be the responsibility of the staff.

The Collections Committee shall

1. annually review the Dyer Library/Saco Museum (DLSM) collections policy and recommend approval to the DLSM board of trustees;
2. provide a community viewpoint and additional expertise in collection matters;
3. meet at least six times per year to discuss acquisitions and deaccessions;
4. work with staff to ensure collections are properly conserved, preserved, secured, and, when necessary, restored;
5. ensure accessibility of the collections to researchers;
6. encourage loans of collection items for exhibitions and educational opportunities;
7. cultivate private individuals and businesses for future donations and bequests;
8. identify objects for possible acquisition or donation; and
9. help the board of trustees to understand collections issues.

Acquisitions and Accessions

First, let us consider the difference between an acquisition and an accession. Three definitions provided by Simmons (2006, 37) should be kept in mind: An acquisition is "something obtained by a museum." An accession, on the other hand, is "an acquisition that a museum formally adds to its collections, to be held in the public trust and administered according to the collections management policy." Finally, accessioning is "the process of transferring ownership of an acquisition to the museum." Generally, objects or other materials going into the museum's permanent collection are accessioned, while material for an education, research, or reference collection is acquired but not accessioned.

Photo 4.1. Abbe Museum Collections Assistant Rosamund Rea preparing to accession baskets into the collection (2001).

With these distinctions in mind, you may want to include both acquisition and accession policies in one section, or you may divide them. That is up to you. This section of your CMP defines what your museum collects and how.

The acquisitions and accessions section of a CMP generally includes the following:

- What items should be acquired to meet your mission? This may be defined by subject matter, geographical area, period, association with individuals or groups, and so on.

- How does your museum acquire collections? This may include such means as gifts or donations, purchases, exchanges, bequests, field collections, and so on.
- Are there legal and ethical criteria for acquisitions or accessions? This generally includes such criteria as clear title, documented provenance, alignment with the museum's mission, and ability to care for the item (textbox 4.5).

If your museum has well-defined criteria for the types of materials it may acquire, such as clear limits in period or provenance, these criteria may also be included (textbox 4.6). You may also want to include the basic accessioning procedures used at your museum and a listing of the necessary paperwork, such as a deed of gift and an accession record.

TEXTBOX 4.5

ABBE MUSEUM COLLECTIONS MANAGEMENT POLICY (EXCERPT)

Acquisition criteria: Library materials and museum objects must meet the following criteria before being acquired by the museum. The collections manager, in consultation with the Collections Committee, shall approve the acquisition of objects that meet the criteria of this policy.

1. The present owner must have clear title.
2. The materials or objects must be documented as to provenance and provenience to the extent possible.
3. All moral, legal, and ethical implications of the acquisition must have been considered.
4. The acquisition's appropriateness, significance, artistic and scientific merit, utility, and condition must have been considered.
5. The acquisition must be consistent with the mission of the Abbe Museum.
6. The museum must be able to care for the acquisition in keeping with professionally accepted standards.
7. Rights, title, and interests to potential acquisitions shall be obtained by the museum free and clear of restrictions. Any exceptions must be considered by the director, collections manager, and Collections Committee and approved by the board of trustees.

TEXTBOX 4.6

GENERAL HENRY KNOX MUSEUM COLLECTIONS MANAGEMENT POLICY (EXCERPT)

II. Acquisitions

A. The collection shall be restricted to objects, documents, or ephemera associated with the period when the Knox family inhabited their home, known as Montpelier (1794–1854), or those associated with the history of the replica built in 1929. The primary emphasis shall be placed on objects with a direct Knox association or from Henry and Lucy's lifetimes (1750–1824). The museum shall not accept objects from later than 1855; those that predate 1750 shall be open to consideration on a case-by-case basis.

Many historical societies and museums that have been in existence for a long period have poorly documented portions of their collections. This often poses a particular challenge in determining the legal status of the objects and establishing clear museum ownership. If you are dealing with a number of these so-called found-in-collections objects, your CMP should address this. Some policies include this in the accessions section, while others may create a separate section, referred to by Simmons as an objects-in-custody section. Some of the questions to address include the following: How will the museum determine clear title? Does your state have an abandoned property law that applies to museum collections? What will you do with objects for which no provenance can be determined or clear title cannot be established?

Deaccessions and Disposal

In an ideal world, a museum's acquisitions and accessions policies and procedures would work so well that it would never need to deaccession anything. But since few of us work in a perfect world, it is important to have a clear and well-considered deaccession policy. Deaccessioning, when done right, ensures that a museum uses its resources in the most responsible way and has a collection best suited to meet its mission.

In your deaccessioning policy, you should define acceptable reasons for deciding to permanently remove something from your collection (textbox 4.7). Some of the standard criteria for deaccessioning include that the object lies outside the museum's mission, has deteriorated to a point that it is no longer of interpretive value, or is a duplicate of another, generally better, piece in the

TEXTBOX 4.7

DYER LIBRARY/SACO MUSEUM
COLLECTIONS POLICY (EXCERPT)

VIII. Deaccessioning

The Dyer Library/Saco Museum (DLSM) collections are held in trust for the public, which the organization exists to serve. Deaccessioning impacts the public's trust. The deaccessioning process shall be deliberate, thoughtful, and thorough. The removal of objects from DLSM's collections has ethical, legal, and financial consequences that shall be taken into consideration by staff, the Collections Committee, and the board of trustees.

A. Criteria for Deaccessioning:

Any or all of the following criteria shall be sufficient for an item to be considered for deaccessioning:

1. The object is an unnecessary duplicate of others in the collection.
2. The object does not fit within the organization's mission or collections policy.
3. The object poses a health hazard.
4. The object has deteriorated beyond a point at which it can be put on public display, conserved, or used for study purposes.
5. The Dyer Library/Saco Museum cannot properly care for the object.

Consideration shall be given to the public trust responsibilities of DLSM.

collection. A couple of special cases for deaccessioning in the museum field today include objects being repatriated through NAGPRA and looted Nazi-era artworks being returned to their original owners or their descendants.

The most common reason for deaccessioning is that most museums, over the years, have ended up with objects irrelevant to their missions. Maybe a previous curator just could not say no to an important museum supporter who wanted to give a special item. Maybe someone dropped an object off at the back door over the weekend—you have no idea who, but it is way outside your mission. Or maybe your mission has changed, and objects once relevant no longer are. Because most museums have limited resources, to best serve the public good, you do not want to expend those resources caring for and managing collections that do not help meet the mission. It is a good idea to review your collection periodically to identify objects that lie outside your mission and can be deaccessioned.

This section should also include a statement about who has the authority to approve deaccessioning and a basic series of steps to complete the process. In most cases, the final decision to deaccession is made by an organization's governing body at the recommendation of the director or curator or the collections committee.

It is helpful to enumerate the means of disposal, or actual physical removal from the collection, once the decision to deaccession has been approved. Preference is generally given to means that will keep the material in the public trust, either through donation to or exchange with another institution. If the decision is made to sell the items, most policies require that the sale be done through public auction so as to avoid any real or perceived conflict of interest. If the object is being deaccessioned because it has deteriorated or been determined to be a fake, actual disposal or destruction is an option. Simmons (2006, 60) clearly outlines generally accepted methods of disposal (table 4.1) and several that are inappropriate (table 4.2).

Finally, most CMPs include a statement about how the proceeds of any sale of deaccessioned collections may be used. The AAM, AASLH, and Association of Art Museum Directors (AAMD) all have issued position papers or other statements regarding this sensitive subject. A good summary of these positions is AAM's "Ethics of Deaccessioning" fact sheet, available from its website. AASLH's "Statement of Professional Standards and Ethics" states, "Collections shall not be deaccessioned or disposed of in order to provide financial support for institutional operations, facilities maintenance or any reason other than preservation or acquisition of collections, as defined by institutional policy."[1] In general, history museums limit the use of proceeds from deaccessioning to either the purchase of new collections or the direct care of existing collections. Direct

Table 4.1. Methods of Disposal of Deaccessioned Collection Objects Generally Considered To Be Appropriate

Method	Comment and Potential Concerns
Exchange	Objects or specimens might be exchanged with another museum or other educational institution.
Transfer	Objects can be transferred to another department within the museum or donated to another nonprofit institution.
Repatriation	Objects or specimens might be deaccessioned for return to the appropriate national government, tribal entity, or cultural group.
Sale at public auction	Sale must be handled by a disinterested third party to avoid a conflict of interests or the appearance of a conflict of interest.
Destruction	Sometimes appropriate for severely deteriorated objects or specimens, fakes, forgeries, or hazardous material. Destruction should be documented and witnessed by an impartial observer.

*Adapted from Simmons 2006: 60, table 8.3

Table 4.2. Methods of Disposal of Deaccessioned Collection Objects Considered To Be Inappropriate

Method	Comments
Sale in the museum shop	This is contrary to professional standards and could be viewed negatively by the press and the public.
Sale to a staff member or a member of the governing authority	This is generally considered to be a bad idea and could be viewed negatively by the press and the public. Some museums allow staff or board members to purchase material at public auction, as long as they have no special knowledge or advantage of the sale.
Transfer to a staff member or a member of the governing authority	This can raise issues of actual or perceived conflict of interests.

*Adapted from Simmons 2006: 60, table 8.4

care may include such things as conservation treatments or new storage cabinets. Art museums, under the guidance of the AAMD, tend to limit deaccessioning proceeds to the purchase of new collections. It is generally agreed that these proceeds should not be used to meet general operating expenses. If they are, then the museum may be expected to capitalize its collections.[2]

The question of how proceeds from the sale of deaccessioned collections objects are used is closely tied to the decision a museum makes about whether to capitalize its collections. We have already talked some about the importance of a museum's holding collections in the public trust. A major point to consider in this regard is whether your collections could be seized as assets and sold to cover debts incurred by the organization. If you capitalize your collections, this becomes a possibility. And if a museum uses the proceeds from the sale of collections for general operating expenses, the Internal Revenue Service (IRS) will likely require that it count its collections as financial assets. Most museums have a policy of not capitalizing their collection. See sources in the bibliography at the end of this chapter to learn more about this often difficult debate.

Loans

Policies for incoming and outgoing loans should be included in your collections management policy. If you do not loan objects from your collections, simply state this fact. This section can be relatively brief, stating the basic parameters for incoming and outgoing loans, with reference to the appropriate documents, or it can list the more detailed requirements that are given in your loan agreement. Table 4.3 provides some criteria to consider, but your institution may need to consider others.

Generally, loan policies should include how loan requests should be made and who makes decisions about loans, both incoming and outgoing (textbox

Table 4.3.   Recommended Criteria for Determining If a Collection Item Is Suitable for Lending to Another Institution

Criteria	Comments
Validation	Does the item have proper documentation?
	Does the item have clear and adequately researched provenance?
	Does the museum have clear title to the item?
Care	Will the item withstand the rigors of packing and shipment?
	Will the item receive adequate care from the borrower?
	Can the item withstand the intended use while on loan?
Use	Is the item needed for a scheduled educational program?
	Is the item an important part of a permanent exhibit installation?
	If the item is requested for research use, is it suitable for the intended purpose?

*Adapted from Simmons 2006: 76, table 9.1

4.8). Loan policies can set a limited period for loans and require regular renewals for extensions beyond this period.

Regarding incoming loans, most museums do not accept long-term loans. Museums occasionally encounter potential donors who want to offer objects or collections as long-term loans in case they change their mind about making the donation; however, this is less than ideal for the museum. You do not want to expend your limited resources to care for something that does not belong to you, only to have it taken back. Many collections management policies will allow for the acceptance of long-term loans in exceptional situations but will require that they be approved by the collections committee or governing body.

Collections Care

In *Things Great and Small*, Simmons (2006) segments several sections related to documenting, caring for, using, and accessing collections (chapters 11 to 14). Smaller museums may find it easier to combine these aspects of collections management into a single section in their policy. For example, the Dyer Library/Saco Museum Collections Policy has a section titled "Collection Management & Care," which includes documentation, preservation and conservation, and risk management. "Access to Collections" is a separate section. As you develop more detailed policies and procedures regarding these various aspects of collections management, you can expand sections or separate topics as needed.

The documentation section may list and describe the required documentation and include policies regarding the use and management of a collections management database, such as PastPerfect. The collections care section generally gives guiding principles for how the museum will care for its collections and generally includes a statement that the museum will follow professionally accepted standards regarding storage, protection, preventative conservation, and

TEXTBOX 4.8

AMERICAN PRECISION MUSEUM COLLECTIONS MANAGEMENT POLICY (EXCERPT)

Lending and Borrowing

Outgoing Loans

The American Precision Museum (APM) may lend collection objects to museums and other suitable institutions for appropriate purposes, such as a special exhibition within the limits of collections care and conservation and the APM's exhibition plans. Normally, objects will be lent only for nonprofit educational and scholarly purposes usually involving research or a public exhibition.

A loan request should be submitted in writing, and an up-to-date facilities report must be on file with the museum. The facilities report should describe the borrowing institution's facilities, staff, security, and environmental controls.

The executive director is responsible for reviewing loan requests. The maximum time frame for a loan agreement is two years, at which time it may be renewed by both parties.

Incoming Loans

The American Precision Museum borrows objects to supplement its collections for exhibition or research purposes. The director initiates loan requests and ensures that proper documentation is maintained.

conservation treatment. You may want to include an integrated pest management policy in this section if you have one.

Risk management refers to institutional policies and physical systems employed to minimize risk to the collections. This may include standard opening and closing procedures to ensure that the building is secure, specifics about security and fire alarm systems, and information about the type and extent of insurance for the collection. Another important part of risk management is emergency preparedness. While it is generally a separate document, you may want to reference your disaster plan in this section.

Access and Use

Museums provide access to their collections in a variety of ways, and it is helpful to have policies in place regarding access and use. The primary form of

Photo 4.2. Collections storage at the original Abbe Museum (2000).

collections access is through exhibition. However, you may also provide access to researchers or students. Definitions of who has access to what and how access is granted are the basic elements of an access policy (textbox 4.9). Access policies can also be different for different categories of your collection. For example, access to permanent collections is generally more limited than access to archives

Photo 4.3. Collections storage at the new Abbe Museum (2008).

and library collections. It is important to strike the right balance between access, security, and preservation.

Access to institutional archives and records and to collections records may be governed by local or state Freedom of Access or Freedom of Information legislation. If so, it is a good idea to include this in your access policy. If you are governed by a government entity, such as a town or county, this may be especially relevant.

TEXTBOX 4.9

DR. POUND HISTORICAL FARMSTEAD COLLECTIONS MANAGEMENT POLICY (EXCERPT)

Access: General Policy and Definitions

The museum's collection is housed in the museum or in storage facilities that the foundation utilizes from time to time. Artifacts are available for public inspection at the museum, subject to the preservation requirements of the artifact and availability of museum staff or volunteers to facilitate the examination of the artifact. Access to the collection must be restricted to ensure the safety of the artifacts from theft, loss, or damage. Appointments for artifact research will be made in advance with the executive director; access is not guaranteed without an appointment. The museum may, at its sole discretion, limit the form of access to artifacts. For extensive use of the museum collection, a researcher is to submit a research proposal prior to the visit. Use of the collections database for research shall be conducted or assisted by the museum staff.

The executive director is responsible for limiting the number of keys and the number of people who have access to the museum outside normal hours of operation. Security at the museum is provided by an electronic alarm system, which includes motion detection. Public access to the property is restricted by a high fence and locked gates. Currently, hours of operation are Tuesday, Wednesday, Thursday, and Saturday from 12 p.m. to 3:00 p.m. or by appointment.

In addition, it may be helpful to clearly state how your collection, or specific categories within it, may be used. Will you permit use of your collections by commercial entities for reproduction? If you have archaeological or natural history collections, will you permit destructive analysis of material from your collection?

Image Use

Many small museums and historical societies have wonderful collections of historic photographs and other images that document the history and culture of a town, state, or region. Having a policy in place regarding the use of the images, both within the institution and by outside users, is important. It is critical to make sure your institution does not violate copyright law in this area, and image-use fees can be a source of income for a small museum. At the same time, a museum wants to fulfill its mission and ensure that its resources are available for educational use when appropriate.

Image-use policies generally define who may use images from a collection, detail how permission and reproductions should be requested, and outline any fees that will be charged. Some organizations may give permission to any individual or organization wishing for it, while others may allow use in research and scholarly publications but not in advertising. Fees are generally set depending on how the image will be used, with a small fee, if any, for educational or nonprofit use and higher fees for commercial uses, such as textbooks, commercial films, or retail products.

Having a good basic knowledge of copyright law is helpful when creating and administering an image-use or rights-and-reproductions policy. A number of resources can help you gain this knowledge. Cornell University provides up-to-date and accessible information through its Copyright Information Center, available online at www.copyright.cornell.edu. Two popular resources provided on this site are the "Copyright Term and the Public Domain in the United States" table and the "Fair Use Checklist." For more detailed information specific to museums, including a number of sample forms and agreements, the AAM has published *A Museum Guide to Copyright and Trademark*.

Ethics

As museums, we rely on the public trust. We need the support and participation of our communities and stakeholders if we are to meet our missions and be financially sustainable. For this reason, museums must be sure to do not only what is legal but also what is ethical.

Some museums have a code of ethics that governs all aspects of their operations, including governance, daily operations, staff, interpretation, and collections management. If you already have an approved code of ethics that addresses collections management, it can be referenced in your CMP and included in the appendices. You may want to reiterate the parts that refer to collections or to elaborate on ethical considerations that are especially important to responsible collections management.

Some ethical issues particular to collections management include the following (Simmons 2006, 149):

- Collecting (ensuring that collections are ethically acquired)
- Conflicts of interest (ensuring that staff and board activities do not conflict with the institution's mission, goals, and interests)
- Personal collecting and personal collections (ensuring that staff and board member collecting does not compete with museum collecting)

- Use of personal collections by staff, volunteers, or board members in museum exhibits and programs
- Storage of personal collections in the museum
- Acquisitions by staff, volunteers, or board members of material deaccessioned from the museum (usually forbidden or strongly discouraged)
- Appraisals and authentications (ensuring compliance with the IRS's ban on museum staff and board members offering appraisals or authentications of objects that may be acquired by the museum)
- Personal activities (ensuring that personal activities of staff and board members do not damage the collections or the intellectual integrity of the collections and the museum)

Both the AASLH and AAM provide guidance to museums on ethical issues. AASLH's "Statement of Professional Standards and Ethics" and associated documents are provided on its website at www.aaslh.org/ethics.htm. The AAM's "Code of Ethics for Museums" is also online at www.aam-us.org/museumresources/ethics/coe.cfm. If your museum focuses on a particular academic discipline, you may also want to consider codes of ethics provided by the appropriate professional organization.

Additional Collections Issues

Some museums may have additional special considerations regarding collections management that should be included in a collections management policy. Depending on the nature of your collections, your CMP may want to address these legal or special ethical requirements:

- Antiquities Act of 1906 (if you have archaeological artifacts found on federal land)
- Archaeological Resources Protection Act of 1979 (if you have archaeological collections from public or tribal lands)
- Native American Graves Protection and Repatriation Act (if you have Native American human remains, grave goods, or archaeological or historic ceremonial objects)
- United Nations Educational, Scientific, and Cultural Organization's Convention on the Means of Prohibiting and Preventing the Illicit Import, Export and Transfer of Ownership of Cultural Property, 1970 (if you have artifacts or other cultural objects from outside the United States, such as Greco-Roman objects or Central or South American archaeological objects)

- Recent developments in Nazi-era provenance research (if you have art created before World War II that came into your collection after that conflict ended and may have been taken from the original owner by the Nazi regime throughout Europe)
- National and international laws and treaties regarding threatened or endangered species (if you have natural history collections or objects made with animal parts such as feathers, fur, teeth, and claws)

Appendices

Appendices should be carefully selected to be relevant to the policy and should be "clearly connected with the sections in the policy that discuss them" (Harmon 2009, 22). This connection can be made with footnotes or other reference formats.

Some of the materials you may want to include as appendices are key collections forms, such as your deed of gift, accession record, loan form, and image-use agreement. Some museums include a glossary of key terms. If related museum policies are referenced in the CMP, it is helpful to include these in your appendices.

Review and Revision

Like any good policy, your collections management policy needs to be kept current. It is a good idea to set a regular schedule for review and possible revision of your CMP; every three years is generally recommended. Changes in staffing, mission, or relevant laws may necessitate more frequent revisions. Also establish who is responsible for reviewing the policy and for making and approving revisions. This is often the responsibility of the collections committee in cooperation with collections staff.

Conclusion

A good collections management policy, written to meet the needs of your organization, is an essential element of professional museum practice. It ensures that your museum is complying with legal requirements and being consistent with the ethics of the field. Your CMP helps you develop and manage your collection in ways that maximize your ability to meet your mission and to tell stories with objects. Once you tackle the task of creating a policy, it will make everyday operations and decisions so much easier and allow all staff and volunteers to follow the included standards and guidelines consistently. You will find it very much worth your while!

Acknowledgments

Special thanks to Elizabeth L. Harmon for sharing her master's thesis, "When Policy Meets Practicality: Creating a Collections Management Policy for a Small Historical Museum." Also, I thank my colleagues who shared their collections management policies and their experiences creating and working with them: Jessica Skwire Routhier, museum director, and Marie O'Brien, collections manager, at the Dyer Library/Saco Museum in Saco, Maine; Ellen Dyer, executive director, and Matthew Hansbury, collections manager, at the General Henry Knox Museum in Thomaston, Maine; Beau Harris, collections manager, at the American Precision Museum, Windsor, Vermont; Dr. Marianne Simmons and Lauren Neugebauer, collections committee members, at the Dr. Pound Historical Farmstead in Dripping Springs, Texas; VivianLea Solek, curatorial and collections management consultant, Monroe, Connecticut; and Laurie Coleman-Snead, Longyear Museum, in Chestnut Hill, Massachusetts.

Bibliography

See the collections management policies of the Abbe Museum (2006), the American Precision Museum (2010), the Dr. Pound Historical Farmstead (2009), the Dyer Library/Saco Museum (2008), and the General Henry Knox Museum (2008).

Resources
American Association for State and Local History (AASLH). *StEPs: Standards and Excellence Program for History Organizations.* Nashville, TN: AASLH, 2009.

Harmon, Elizabeth L. "When Policy Meets Practicality: Creating a Collections Management Policy for a Small Historical Museum." Master's thesis, University of Washington, 2009.

Simmons, John E. *Things Great and Small: Collections Management Policies.* Washington, DC: American Association of Museums, 2006.

Additional Resources
Buck, Rebecca A., and Jean Allman Gilmore. *Collection Conundrums: Solving Collections Management Mysteries.* Washington, DC: American Association of Museums, 2007.

——, eds. *Museum Registration Methods.* 5th ed. Washington, DC: American Association of Museums, 2010.

Gardner, James B., and Elizabeth E. Merritt. *The AAM Guide to Collections Planning.* Washington, DC: American Association of Museums, 2004.

Malaro, Marie C. *A Legal Primer on Managing Museum Collections.* Washington, DC: Smithsonian Institution Press, 1998.

Porter, Daniel R. *Current Thoughts on Collections Policy: Producing the Essential Documents for Administering Your Collections.* American Association for State and Local History (AASLH) Technical Report 1. Nashville, TN: AASLH, 1985.

Steiner, Christine, Michael Shapiro, and Brett I. Miller. *A Museum Guide to Copyright and Trademark.* Washington, DC: AAM, 1999.

Notes

1. American Association for State and Local History, *Statement of Professional Standards and Ethics, Adopted 6/02,* http://www.aaslh.org/documents/AASLHProfessional-StandardsandEthics.pdf (accessed October 7, 2011).

2. William G. Tompkins, "Should Museums Capitalize Their Collections? Or How Much Collateral Is in That Caravaggio?" *Museum News* (January–February 2004), www.aam-us.org/pubs/mn/MN_JF04_LawEthics.cfm.

COLLECTIONS PLANNING: BEST PRACTICES IN COLLECTIONS STEWARDSHIP

Nicolette B. Meister and Jackie Hoff

It has come to be recognized that a collection should not be made hap-hazard, but should have some definite purpose, and the specimens of which it is composed be parts of a connected and consistent whole.

—Frederick A. Lucas, "The Evolution of the Museum," 1907

In 1907 Frederick A. Lucas of the Brooklyn Institute of Arts and Sciences presented a paper titled "The Evolution of the Museum" at the second annual meeting of the American Association of Museums (AAM). He traced the evolution of museums and museum collections and laid out the importance of purposeful collections. Lucas compared "haphazard" collecting to the activity of a stamp collector who "has no end in view other than to obtain as many different stamps as possible" (1907, 88). A hundred years later, the message is still relevant, and time has exacerbated the pitfalls of haphazard collecting. Lucas also told his audience, "A collection of specimens does not make a museum any more than a collection of paints and brushes makes an artist," and "the true value of a museum does not lie in its specimens alone, but in what it does or what is done with them" (1907, 89). Collections planning articulates the purpose of our collections and how they are best used to meet our missions and the needs of our audiences. A collections plan guides the content and development of a museum's collection over a period and identifies the resources available to accomplish the established priorities. The outcome of collections planning is a set of collecting goals that ensure what we do with our collections has value to the communities we serve.

The words "museum" and "institution" are used interchangeably throughout this chapter to encompass a broad range of organizations, including history museums; historic houses and sites; science, technology, and nature centers; and zoos, arboretums, planetariums, and botanical gardens. Historically, their relationship with objects has differentiated these institutions from other scientific, educational, and aesthetic organizations. Despite the fact that "10 percent of museums identify themselves as not owning or using collections" (Merritt 2008, 3),[1] the vast majority of the approximately 17,500[2] museums in the United States do care for, own, or use collections to educate and inspire, make meaning, and draw connections between the past and present. For many institutions, collections can present as many opportunities as barriers to advancement of the mission and to public service. Standards and best practices exist for how best to care for and manage collections, but in the last ten years, attention has turned to a critical examination of the content of collections in order to identify strengths and weaknesses and to plan strategies for control of museum collections.

Since Lucas's 1907 paper was written, museums and their collections have evolved and continued to grow and are now guided by professional standards and practices for all aspects of operation. Despite these guidelines, collections frequently have grown without "some definite purpose" often due to the perception that it is better to take things than to offend a donor. Legacy collections, which may date to a museum's founding or stem from the collecting focus of past directors or curators, and unsolicited donations are a part of most collections, but we are now predisposed to question how these objects connect to the mission and to clarify the rationale behind the "consistent whole" (i.e., the collection). Whether the objects that make up an institution's collections are living or nonliving or part of the permanent, research, or educational collections, they are held in the public trust and, as such, should advance the institution's mission and serve the public at large.

The late Victorian era was a period of great museum building and prolific collecting in the United States. Early collections were meant to represent complete "encyclopedias" of the world. Collecting was often opportunistic. Collections were often built through "passive collecting"—that is, simply accepting what was offered. Our legacy of collecting is visible today in the over 4.8 billion artifacts held in trust by more than thirty thousand archives, historical societies, libraries, museums, scientific research collections, and archaeological repositories in the United States.[3] With so many objects in so many institutions, it is not surprising that less than 5 percent are exhibited at any one time. And our nation's collections are growing. Marjorie Schwarzer (2006, 71) reports that "the aggregate rate of collection growth is 1 to 5 percent annually: millions of additional objects each year." As collections continue to grow, so do the costs of preservation, management, and access. Twenty years ago, the direct and indirect operating costs of collections management and care averaged about $240 per square meter (Lord 1989); costs have certainly increased since then. The high cost of collecting is just one of many reasons why collections planning and selective acquisition are vital to sustainability and maintaining intellectual and physical control over collections.

Through the AAM's accreditation process, members of the Accreditation Commission are able to assess the health of U.S. museums. The process affords opportunities to identify strengths and weaknesses and to bring issues to the surface through discussions at national conferences, seminars, and colloquia. In the early 2000s, the commission reported that over 25 percent of accreditation applications were tabled because of inadequacies in collections stewardship (Sullivan 2004, 1). While some of the postponing actions were a direct result of low levels of documentation or poor storage conditions, "The Accreditation Commission has identified a pattern of recurring problems connected to collections stewardship and institutional planning: insufficient resources to support collections; collections unrelated to the institution's mission; and a lack of integration between planning for collections, interpretation, and facilities" (Gardner and Merritt 2004, 33). In addition, the 2007 Forum on Historic Sites Stewardship in the 21st Century found that "undefined collecting coupled with a lack of professional standards and inconsistent practices regarding deaccessioning are an impediment to change and sustainability" (Vaughan 2008, 7). Both findings clearly identify and articulate the problem at hand. Collections in museums across the country have grown without purpose, limited resources (human and financial) are being used to maintain collections irrelevant to institutional missions, and museums lack a vision for future uses of collections. The museum landscape is changing rapidly as a result of fluctuating attendance and financial instability. All aspects of a museum's operations must have intentionality[4] and be sustainable in order to remain relevant and responsive to communities in the twenty-first century. Significant resources are devoted to acquisition, management, and care of collections, so why do we not devote the same amount of effort to planning what goes into our collections and questioning how our collections serve our mission and audience?

It is pretty easy to understand the problem and to support the call for change, but adding yet another benchmark for best practice might seem like an unobtainable ideal. We have collections management policies and procedures, preservation plans, strategic plans, and interpretive plans, and now the field wants us to add collections plans? And just what is the difference between a collections management policy and a collections plan? Do we really need both? And yes, policies and planning are never finished (that is the nature of the beast), so the idea of adding yet another kind of plan to the agenda does seem overwhelming—especially to the small museum professional. Small museums frequently operate with a small staff juggling multiple responsibilities and often employ volunteers to perform key staff functions.[5] Any staff member with knowledge of the collections—whether a part-time volunteer or a full-time curator—can initiate the collections planning process, and we hope to show you that it does not have to be an ordeal. We hope that by the end of this chapter, you will not only understand what a collections plan is but also feel motivated to apply collections planning strategies to your institution because, in the long run, collections planning helps to make all aspects of a museum's operation more cohesive by articulating a shared vision and strategic objectives.

Collections Stewardship Responsibilities: Cutting through the Jargon

One characteristic of a profession is a shared language or jargon. We find ourselves using our professional jargon in everyday conversation, but how many of us can easily define these specialized concepts? Because these terms are central to our discussion of collections planning, a clear understanding of their roots and meaning is essential. Thus, to understand why collections planning has emerged as a best practice in collections stewardship, it is important to revisit several topics: the fundamentals of trust organizations and their impact on collections stewardship; the difference between standards and best practices and by what means they are established; how standards and best practices are implemented through collections policies, procedures, and plans; and why these standards and best practices are important to small institutions.

Museums hold collections in trust for the public. Because most museums are nonprofit and generally classified as charitable corporations or charitable trusts, they are held to a much higher standard of care and degree of responsibility than for-profit organizations. Such trust relationships come with a number of important responsibilities: duty of care, duty of loyalty, and duty of obedience. These duties exist to ensure that the beneficiaries (the public) of trust-like organizations maintain trust and confidence in the institution. Duty of care requires that staff and board members perform their duties in good faith, with a reasonable amount of due diligence and care, and do not endanger assets (funds or collections) by making poor decisions or taking undue risks. Duty of loyalty requires that staff and board members put the interests of the museum before their personal interests and the interests of third parties; in short, museums must avoid conflicts of interest and decision-making should be guided by what is best for the museum, not oneself. Duty of obedience requires that staff and board members be true to the mission of the organization (Malaro 1998, 6–7). "Doing a lot poorly or favoring peripheral activities for short-term benefits calls into question proper adherence to the duty of obedience" (Malaro 2002, 73). Good collections stewardship requires that staff and board members understand and uphold their fiduciary (trust) responsibilities to preserve, care for, and provide access to collections for the benefit of the public.

In 2005 the AAM Accreditation Commission's revised expectations regarding collections stewardship became effective. Public trust and accountability became prominent characteristics (Buck and Gilmore 2007, 79). Textbox 5.1, taken from *National Standards and Best Practices for U.S. Museums* (Merritt 2008), details the AAM's Characteristics of Excellence for U.S. Museums standards for collections stewardship.

These standards of collections stewardship are the fundamental guiding principles that apply to all museums considered collecting institutions. The AAM posted these standards in "plain English" to make the message clearer: "Know what stuff you have, know what stuff you need, know where it is, take good care of it, make sure someone gets some good out of it, especially people you care about and your neighbors."[6] At the core of these standards is the basic idea that collections must benefit the institution's mission and serve the public at large. These standards should inform the collections planning process. Standards are best thought of as big-picture principles akin to ethics. Ethical standards are not like legal standards that prescribe what one can and cannot do. Ethical standards advise what one should and should not do. Standards are voluntarily assumed, are often more demanding than legal requirements, have no enforcement mechanisms, and depend on professional education and peer pressure. "*Standards* are generally accepted levels of attainment that all museums are expected to achieve. *Best practices* are commendable actions and philosophies that demonstrate an awareness of standards, successfully solve problems, can

---

TEXTBOX 5.1

CHARACTERISTICS OF EXCELLENCE FOR U.S. MUSEUMS, STANDARDS FOR COLLECTIONS STEWARDSHIP

- The museum owns, exhibits, or uses collections that are appropriate to its mission.
- The museum legally, ethically, and effectively manages, documents, cares for, and uses the collections.
- The museum's collections-related research is conducted according to appropriate scholarly standards.
- The museum strategically plans for the use and development of its collections.
- Guided by its mission, the museum provides public access to its collections while ensuring their preservation.

be replicated and that museums may choose to emulate if appropriate to their circumstances" (Merritt 2008, 6).

Best practices are exemplary actions that take standards to a higher level of implementation. "Best practices are 'extra credit.' Museums deserve applause if they can implement them but shouldn't be faulted if they can't" (Merritt 2008, 6). Standards and best practices are often used interchangeably, but it is important to recognize that while standards are expected, best practice represents goals that may be unrealistic or inappropriate for some institutions. National collections stewardship standards do not call for all museums to have a collections plan, as this is still considered best practice. However, having a collections plan in place will certainly help an institution plan strategically for the use and development of its collections, which is one of the collections stewardship standards listed in textbox 5.1.

The museum profession is ever evolving, so the standards and best practices that guide it have changed over time. The origins of these standards and best practices are rooted in the field itself. National organizations, such as the AAM and the American Association for State and Local History (AASLH), continue to solicit feedback and debate about standards through programs such as the AAM's Accreditation Program and the AASLH's Standards and Excellence Program for History Organizations.[7] Feedback from the field comes through national and regional conferences and colloquia.

Collections Management Policies, Procedures, and Plans

Responsible collections stewardship requires museums to have a system in place to establish collections control and accountability. This system consists of collections management policies that guide core functions, including acquisitions, accessions, deaccessions, loans, documentation systems, and access to and use of collections. A collections management policy is actually a set of multiple policies that "govern what a museum does to care for and grow its collections and make them available to the public" (Simmons 2006, 2). A collections policy is an essential document because it sets the standards for exercising good judgment, provides guidelines and principles that regulate activities, and gives staff the authority to implement the policy. Policy guidelines are modeled after the standards set by the field (i.e., the AAM's Characteristics of Excellence for U.S. Museums) and tend to vary little from museum to museum (Gardner and Merritt 2004, 13). See chapter 4 in this book, in addition to John Simmons's *Things Great and Small: Collections Management Policies* (2006) and Marie C. Malaro's *A Legal Primer on Managing Museum Collections* (1998) for more information on collections management policies.

Collections procedures are a separate document that provides step-by-step how-to instructions or protocols for implementing the guidelines set forth in the collections policy. Procedures include functions such as cataloging, marking objects with numbers, and documenting collections. Daniel B. Reibel's *Registration Methods for the Small Museum* (2008) and Rebecca A. Buck and Jean Allman Gilmore's *Museum Registration Methods*, 5th edition (2010) are good examples of essential museum texts concerned primarily with collection procedures. In addition to the above references, Simmons (2006) and Buck and Gilmore (2007) provide thorough discussions of the differences between policy and procedure.

So how does a collections plan differ from a collections management policy? A plan is really just a set of intended actions to accomplish a specific goal. Policy, on the other hand, is not action oriented. Policies identify rules and guidelines that inform and regulate our decisions and actions. Plans are time limited because they dictate what will be accomplished over a specific period, by whom, using what resources. Policy, on the other hand, is not inherently time limited. Policies change as standards in the field evolve (Gardner and Merritt 2004, 13), but the basic principles that govern policy (duty of care, loyalty, and obedience) are constant. Table 5.1 provides a side-by-side comparison of the differences between a collections plan and a collections policy. James Gardner and Elizabeth Merritt (2004, 26) also offer a useful table for comparing the differences between policies and plans. It is important to know the difference between a policy and a plan before writing or revising either.

Despite the differences, there is some overlap between a collections management policy and a collections plan. Both include a collections overview or scope of collections and outline accession and deaccession criteria. However, at the heart of a plan is an institutionally specific intellectual framework that identifies the museum's collecting goals. A collections plan assesses the relative strengths

Table 5.1. Differences between Collections Plans and Collections Policies

Collections Plan	Collections Policy
Action oriented—identifies what actions will be taken to accomplish goals and by whom and with what resources	Not action oriented—grounded in rules and guidelines that inform and regulate what we do
Intellectual framework is institutionally specific	Content based on standards shared by most institutions
Time limited	Not time limited—change as standards in the field evolve
Analysis of existing collections—assesses strengths and weaknesses and identifies gaps, overlaps, and over-representation	Scope of collections—brief and summative
Outcome oriented—priorities and strategies (actions) that reinforce the intellectual framework	Framework for decision-making: reference tool

and weaknesses of the collections, identifying gaps that align with the collecting goals and areas of overrepresentation or overlap with the collections of peer institutions. As a result of assessment and reevaluation, the plan may include specific priorities for acquisitions and deaccessions and will articulate strategies (actions) for implementation. The plan provides a more in-depth, detailed assessment of the collections and frames the scope of collections around the collecting goals. The collections plan will also map the financial, physical, and staff resources needed to achieve the collecting goals (Simmons 2006, 7).

The scope of collections in a collections management policy will be much broader and provide a brief overview of the collections, their history, and criteria for accessions and deaccessions. A policy will state the legal and ethical guidelines that regulate acquisitions and deaccessions and are grounded in the standards for excellence in collections stewardship. As such, much of the content of collections policies will be similar between institutions. Because of the likelihood for overlap between collections policies and plans, each document should reference the other.

Why Do Small Museums Need Collections Plans?

Standards and best practices are important to small museums for a number of reasons. It is not uncommon for the staff and volunteers of small museums to feel isolated from the larger museum community. Small museums are more likely to be located in rural areas, and it is often difficult for small museum professionals to participate in professional conferences—not just for financial reasons but also because we are often the only staff members at our institutions and thus cannot take time away for professional development. Regardless of the size of the institution, professional standards are shared throughout the museum field because they reflect areas of broad agreement. Standards help us measure our goals and performance against the norms of our peers. Standards also provide an opportunity to network and build communities of peer institutions by problem solving as a team to resolve common issues.

Understanding of and adherence to standards is also of critical importance to public opinion within our communities. Public trust must be earned. The collections stewardship standards reviewed in this chapter exist to help prevent museums from finding themselves in compromising situations that might cause the public to question how they care for objects, how they uphold ethical and legal obligations, and their motives. The public expects that donated objects will be cared for, documented, interpreted, and displayed. Practicing transparency in all aspects of operations helps to build public trust. When museums are seen as behaving responsibly, support is more easily solicited. There is no enforcement mechanism for adherence to standards, but unethical behavior can reduce attendance, contributions, and tax support.

Every year, billions of dollars of taxpayers' money and private funds are administered by museums to support core activities, including preservation, education, and interpretation. Evidence that an institution practices and is committed to good collections stewardship is critical to the success of many federal and state grant applications. Because standards provide benchmarks for generally acceptable levels of attainment, grant reviewers are often instructed to look for evidence that the institution is practicing good, responsible collections care. For small museums that have a difficult time saying no to undesirable objects offered for donation or find themselves the unwanted beneficiaries of doorstep donations, collections planning can provide some solace. One of the goals of collections planning is to develop strategies for collecting to clarify what is and is not needed and the delineating criteria. It is much easier to say no when you can put personal feelings aside and provide a rationale and basis for your decision. This ability can empower staff and serve as a valuable learning opportunity for potential donors. Museums are not warehouses. By explaining the importance of collections stewardship and selective acquisition, the museum is practicing transparency, and the public is more likely to respect the museum's decision and to lend support in ways that meet strategic objectives.

Collections planning "has begun to emerge as essential best practice for museums" (Gardner and Merritt 2004, 1). Bearing in mind the difference between standards and best practice, institutions should strive to undertake collections planning. Though not currently an expectation, a collections plan will one day likely be a required document for AAM accreditation. The majority of U.S. museums, however, still do not undertake the accreditation process. In fact, only 5 percent of all U.S. museums are accredited by the AAM.[8] The importance of collections planning lies not in the professional capital it may buy an institution but in its ability to help a museum remain true to its mission. Indiscriminate growth is neither viable nor sustainable. The collections planning process provides the framework for making strategic decisions about collections.

Collections Planning, or Know What Stuff You Need

Collections planning is about thinking and acting strategically to acquire, develop, and allocate collection resources to advance the mission of the museum. According to John Simmons, "A good collections plan helps a museum remain true to its mission without amassing a lot of junk; without it, the museum's collecting activities will lack control" (2006, 3). Books by Simmons (2006) and Buck and Gilmore (2007) have brought focus to the two pillars of collections management: accessibility and control of collections. Accessibility of collections is realized both physically and intellectually. Physical accessibility refers to how collections are stored and the ease of access to collections in storage. Intellectual accessibility refers to how collection information is managed and made accessible through legal documentation, cataloging, and computerization of collection records. Control of collections is about making conscious choices about what an institution does and does not collect. Being in control of, or intentional about, collections means that those who work in an institution (1) continually question and clarify how the collections are being used, (2) have a holistic understanding of the collections they curate and the relative strengths and weaknesses of the collections, and (3) can describe where the collections should grow or be culled to best serve the needs of the institution. For these reasons, the collections plan should be tied to an institution's strategic, interpretive, or research plans.

Components of a Collections Plan

With online access to limitless resources, it is tempting to start the search for information about the components of a collections plan by simply googling "museum collections plan." The first hit will point you to the AAM website, an essential resource. Before you start to concern yourself too much with what goes into the plan, it is a good idea first to gather examples from institutions like yours. If you are a member of the AAM, you can access its Information Center, which provides a wealth of information and access to its sample document collection. When requesting sample collections plans, be sure to indicate your institution's discipline, budget size, and governance structure so the AAM can identify plans that best fit your institution. The AAM's pool of sample documents is growing, so it will likely be able to send four or five examples for you to review. If you are not an AAM member, examples of plans are included in the appendix to Gardner and Merritt's *The AAM Guide to Collections Planning* (2004), and a number of examples are also available online.[9] The AAM Information Center also has three fact sheets on collections planning: "Outline for a Collections Plan," "Creating an Intellectual Framework for Collections Planning," and "Collections Planning: Strategies for Planning and Implementation."[10] "Collections Planning: Strategies for Planning and Implementation" is particularly useful as it provides good tips on how to begin the process.

In response to concerns about indiscriminate collections growth, in 2002 the AAM and the National Museum of American History sponsored the National Collections Colloquium, which brought together eighty museum professionals from thirty-six institutions of different types and sizes from across the United States. The colloquium sought to identify who is doing collections planning,

TEXTBOX 5.2

SAMPLE OUTLINE FOR A COLLECTIONS PLAN

- Executive summary
- Preamble
  - Purpose of the collections plan
  - Audience for the document
  - Authority (how the plan was developed, who participated, who wrote it)
- Setting the stage
  - Museum mission or statement of purpose
  - Museum vision
  - Overview of major points of current strategic plan
  - Relationship of collections plan to other museum policy and planning documents
- Intellectual framework (vision for the collection)
- Analysis of existing collections
  - Description/scope
  - History
  - Strengths and weaknesses (gap analysis)
  - Connections to other institutions and their collections
- Shaping the ideal collection
  - Priorities for acquisition and deaccessioning
  - Strategies for acquisition and deaccessioning
  - Criteria for acquisition and deaccessioning
- Implementation strategy
  - Action steps
  - Time line
  - Assignment of responsibilities
- Evaluation
- Reviewing the plan

what the key components are, how to build an intellectual framework or vision that guides collections, and what barriers to collections planning exist in the field. Gardner and Merritt's *The AAM Guide to Collections Planning* is based on the results of the colloquium and is an essential resource for any institution undertaking the collections planning process. The outline of a collections plan presented in textbox 5.2 is taken from that guide. According to Gardner and Merritt, "Not all plans contain all the elements described here, and there is no standard for what goes in which section, the names of the sections, or their order of appearance" (2004, 11). As you review other institutions' collections plans, you may be surprised to discover that they are all different in style and format and can vary in length from six to over thirty pages. Think of these documents not as templates into which you simply insert your institution's name but rather as models of how the different components of a collections plan can be arranged and addressed. Pick the components that are most relevant or essential to your institution. You can always go back and add more sections later. Because plans are time sensitive, the document should be reviewed and likely modified on an annual basis. Also, when considering which components to include in the plan, think about its intended audience. You may decide to create different versions that include more or less detail, depending on whether the plan will be posted online, presented to prospective donors, or used by staff. For example, the Sachse Historical Society developed a collections plan but only posted target areas of desired collections growth and a brief synopsis of the meaning and significance of collections planning on its website (see textbox 5.3).

There are three ways to approach the collections planning process. The first is bottom-up planning. This approach usually starts with initiation of the process by one staff member or a small team of staff members who form a committee that will solicit diverse input. Planning by committee will be slow going, but this model is most likely to result in buy-in because it is not an administrative mandate and provides an opportunity for multiple voices to be heard. The second approach, top-down planning, is usually initiated by a director. This approach tends to be much faster because it includes fewer viewpoints. Another approach growing in popularity is the use of a consultant. Consultants serve as mediators and bring expert advice and an outside perspective. They can organize and guide the committee meetings and write drafts, which will save a great deal of staff time. However, they are also likely to be less familiar with the collections and history of the institution. Regardless of which approach makes the most sense for your museum, institutional commitment is essential. Collections planning does not occur in isolation. It might be initiated by one individual, but ultimately it will require input from other staff and board members. Institutional and staff buy-in will also impact how long the process takes. Also keep in mind that collections planning is time-consuming and labor-intensive. We all juggle multiple responsibilities and often multiple projects, so make sure you are able to carve out time to work on the plan.

Your collections plan might start with an executive summary, which is a brief overview of the major strategies and priorities that will result from the collections planning process. Keep the executive summary short and concise and not laden with jargon. Because it encapsulates the entire plan, it should be written last. Next comes the preamble, an introduction to and explanation

TEXTBOX 5.3

EXAMPLE OF ABBREVIATED COLLECTIONS PLAN POSTED ONLINE

Museum Collection Guidelines

The Sachse Historical Society Board of Directors is working very hard to keep our museum something to be proud of. Many people have generously donated objects and collectible items for the museum and funds that keep it going. It is a very small building, however, and in the interest of keeping the collection relevant and refined, collection guidelines have been developed.

These guidelines will help us determine which things offered to accept and which to decline. They will expand the value of the collection in a predetermined way and will help us pinpoint the areas in which we need to actively expand.

For your reference and for future donations, an abbreviated form of the guidelines is reprinted here. You may read the full collection plan at the museum or by contacting any board member. If you would like to discuss the guidelines or make recommendations, your input is welcome, for they are amendable and flexible.

1. The target areas of the museum will be defined as follows:
   - pre-1854 interpretation
   - 1854–1987 collection of objects in the museum, plus interpretation
   - post-1987 interpretation
2. Criteria for acquisition and retention of objects include the following:
   - historical significance
   - connection to Sachse or the community or state
   - condition
   - object integrity
   - clear title
   - potential for interpretive use
   - relation to people, places, or events in Sachse's past
   - relation to current collection
   - relation to other state or regional collections

of the plan's purpose. Many readers will be unfamiliar with collections plans and much of the terminology used. For this reason, include a definition of a collections plan and definitions of other terms used throughout the plan.[11] The purpose of your plan could be not only to guide future acquisitions but to align collecting strategies with a new mission or collecting focus. The preamble should also identify the document's intended audience and describe the process the institution underwent to develop the plan. It is not a bad idea to get in the habit of compiling minutes from collections planning meetings; these will be valuable sources of information and will demonstrate staff input in the process. The next section of the plan should include your institution's mission and vision statements, an overview of the major points of the current strategic plan, and a discussion of the relationship of the collections plan to other documents, like the collections management policy.

The heart of the collections plan is the intellectual framework. The intellectual framework is the key to maintaining intellectual control over your museum's collections, which, as previously noted, is the main purpose of collections planning. The intellectual framework "provides the compelling vision of why the museum collects what it does, why that is so important and exciting, and why the museum is uniquely suited to fill this role" (Gardner and Merritt 2004, 18). Individual staff members might have intellectual control over the collections, but the plan will help staff and other stakeholders work together to develop a unified voice and set of strategies and priorities to guide the collections.

Start with a review of your institution's mission statement. In order to know what stuff you need, you must have a clearly delineated mission statement. The mission statement guides museum activities and decisions and is the foundation upon which the intellectual framework of the collections plan is built. It is impossible to know what collections you need if there is no shared vision of what the institution does, for whom, and why. All aspects of the museum's operations should be integrated and focused on meeting its mission. You might consider reviewing the last five years' worth of accessions to assess how well acquisitions have served the mission. How have these acquisitions served the needs of research, exhibition, and interpretation? The answer to this question might help you better understand what drives collecting at your institution. Ideally, the intellectual framework should bridge the mission, the collections, and collecting (Gardner and Merritt 2004, 6). The intellectual framework may appear in your collections plan in the form of a vision statement for the collections, a set of parameters regarding what you do and do not collect, or a set of themes central to your institution's mission, or it can be organized by different types of collections your institution houses. The intellectual framework may appear as its own section or be incorporated into other parts of the document. The intellectual framework should answer the question "Where are we going?" and anticipate future uses of the collections (Gardner and Merritt 2004, 18).

The intellectual framework is built through an analysis of the existing collections. This starts with a historical overview of the institution and how the collections were formed. One of the most time-consuming elements of a collections plan is the analysis of the strengths and weaknesses of existing collections. The analysis also sets priorities and strategies for augmenting strengths and addressing weaknesses. This section requires input from everyone who works with collections. That might be just you, or you might have the help of a volunteer, board member, or other staff member. There is no universal criterion to determine whether your collections are strong or weak. Each museum must decide this for itself because value is intrinsically linked to mission. For example, natural history museums consider the duplication of specimens a strength because a large data set is necessary for research purposes. For a history museum, however, owning twenty chairs from the same period might be seen as a weakness because having more does not necessarily increase the exhibition or interpretive value of the collection.

You will also need to look critically at how collections have been used. If portions of your collection have not seen the light of day by way of exhibition, interpretation, or research for decades, it might be time to reconsider their value to your institution (see photo 5.1). Most curators will have a good sense of what is used and what is not. If you have a collections management policy, you can make use of the accession criteria that it should enumerate. These criteria can be a valuable lens through which to examine legacy collections. In addition, consider asking members of your collections planning committee and staff what

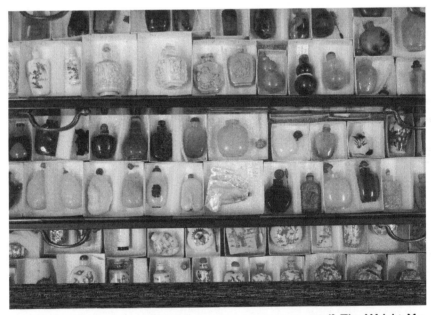

Photo 5.1. How many snuff bottles does one museum need? The Wright Museum of Art recently assessed the scope and content of their Asian snuff bottle collection to reduce redundancy and refine quality. This effort helped the museum to more effectively meet its teaching mission. (Courtesy of the Wright Museum of Art, Beloit College, Beloit, Wisconsin)

they think the perfect collection would look like. What would make that collection perfect? We all know that no one museum can collect everything, but we think less often about the logic of peer institutions with shared audiences that maintain similar collections. For this reason, the analysis should also look outside the institution to identify complementary collections to avoid competition or duplication of effort.

The hard questions that result from this analysis include, but are not limited to, if and how legacy collections serve the current mission and whether you should work to build on current strengths or build strengths in new areas. What do you want the vision of the collections to be now and in the foreseeable future? What do you have, what do you want, and what are your gaps? These are all pretty big questions on their own, never mind as a complete plan. Try to tackle these questions in small increments, and set the plan up to achieve a series of smaller goals. Criteria and priorities should become clearer as you move through the analysis.

For each type of collection, the plan should describe priorities and strategies for acquiring additional material, deaccessioning existing material, or keeping the collection as it is (Gardner and Merritt 2004, 21). These priorities and strategies will help to shape your institution's ideal collection. The priorities might explicitly state what the museum needs (i.e., its gaps) or does not need (i.e., items it should deaccession). The collection strategies are a set of action steps that outline how the museum will accomplish its goals and priorities. If a priority is to fill specific gaps in the collection, will the museum solicit donations for those objects or build an acquisition fund to purchase them? The strategies might reflect the current market (i.e., the availability of certain types of objects), the availability of acquisition funds, or legal considerations, or it might recommend consolidation of certain collections or partnerships with peer institutions. Strategies should include action steps, assign responsibilities for these actions, identify existing or needed resources to accomplish the goals, and provide a time line for completion (Gardner and Merritt 2004, 23).

Textbox 5.4 presents two examples of priorities and strategies from the collections plans of two very different museums. The first example is from a university art museum collections plan organized by type of collection. The analysis of each type of collection is organized into three sections. The section titled "Current State of the Collection" identifies strengths and weaknesses and makes clear that the collection is being used. Under "Factors to Be Considered," potential resources are identified, and purchase is considered the most reasonable strategy for collections growth in this area. The recommendation, or strategy, is to purchase one important work in this area. Strategies for maximizing purchasing power are identified in a different section of the plan. In the second example, a historical society conveys strengths and weaknesses through section headers labeled "Have"

CHAPTER FIVE

EXAMPLES OF COLLECTION PRIORITIES AND STRATEGIES

Smith College Museum of Art Collecting Plan, 2005–2009
<u>B. Medieval Art</u>
Current State of the Collection

The museum has a small collection of medieval stone and wood religious sculptures of good quality. A South German Lamentation group, given in 1997, is a strong addition. Other highlights include a German lindenwood angel and a Flemish Saint John, also in wood; a Romanesque St. Peter from Sarlat; a French Saint Catherine of the second half of the fourteenth century; a Madonna and Child from Lorraine in the International Style. A German sculpture of St. George/St. Michael is a promised gift. In 1991 the museum purchased an intricately carved rosary bead, but it has made no purchases in the medieval field since then. The museum has one fine ivory but little in the way of medieval metalwork, enamels, vessels, jewelry, or architectural ornaments. It has almost no secular art of the period in any medium. There is little languishing in the basement.

Factors To Be Considered

We are aware of one or two sculptures in alumnae hands that may be destined for the museum, but this is not apparently an area in which there is much prospect of encouraging alumnae gifts. If we are to expand our holdings, it will need to be done primarily through purchase.

A faculty member who currently teaches medieval art specializes in manuscript illumination and has expressed interest in having the museum acquire material of this kind. This might present an opportunity for a joint purchase with the Rare Book Room. Another faculty member is also interested in reliquaries.

Medieval art is currently less expensive than, for example, nineteenth- or twentieth-century painting. Objects of quality can be acquired within the museum's price range. With the hiring of a medievalist, there is now greater expertise on staff, so this is an area we should again consider.

The Mount Holyoke College Art Museum is the only other institution in the valley displaying medieval art. It has a small but good collection, a mix of sculptures and decorative arts objects.

Recommendation

Look for opportunities, especially in the area of enamels, metalwork, and other decorative arts. Make one important purchase in this area.

Rogers Historical Museum Permanent Collection Collecting Plan, 2002
Specific Collecting Recommendations
Costumes

Have: christening gowns, some wedding gowns, some handkerchiefs, Red Cross uniform, some military uniforms, Civil War coat (?), aprons, shawls

Need: items from Benton County; clothing: men's formal and everyday, children's everyday, women's everyday; deep mourning; wedding gowns; handkerchiefs; civilian uniforms: business, city (fire, police), organizational; military uniforms: Civil War, Spanish-American War, World War I (Navy, Marine, Air Force), World War II Air Force, Korea, Vietnam, Desert Storm; all types of clothing from the last half of the twentieth century; Quinceañera dress; modern T-shirts

and "Need." This is a very simple, yet effective, way to communicate what you have and what is needed to grow the collections in predetermined ways.

Evaluation and review of the plan are the final two components of the collections plan. Periodic evaluation is necessary to determine if the plan is succeeding. This is most easily done by comparing what has been accomplished with the established action steps and time line for implementation. If the plan is not working effectively, revise it and address the barriers to implementation. Considering all the time and labor you put into the plan, the last thing you want to do is put it on a shelf, never to be used. The plan will no doubt be referenced when pondering new acquisitions and in talking with administrators and donors. It will become a valuable fundraising tool because it brings to light the real and hidden costs of collecting. When offered a collection, you will be more inclined and better positioned to ask for a financial gift to help cover the costs of managing it, because you will be more aware of all the resources needed to care for collections. The plan will also be useful in helping new staff understand your past, present, and future goals. How often the plan is revised will differ for every institution. It may take many years to realize the museum's vision for the collection, but the plan should be reviewed annually to update the time line and celebrate accomplishments. To remind yourself and staff about plan reviews, it is a good idea to put a review-by date on the front page of the document.

Collections Planning in the Real World

Unfortunately, there are as many barriers to collections planning as there are positive outcomes that result from the process. To better understand the barriers, we developed a survey about collections planning and circulated it over museum-related e-mail lists during the summer of 2009.[12] Individuals from thirty-five institutions responded. Most were from history museums (46 percent) with annual budgets between $250,000 and $500,000 (28 percent) and a staff size of between zero and five (43 percent). Fifty-six percent of respondents were in the process of drafting a plan, which they expected to take an average of six to twelve months to complete. Only 21 percent of respondents reported completed plans that were being actively implemented. The survey identified the most widely shared barriers to collections planning as setting priorities and strategies for acquisition and deaccession. See textbox 5.4 for examples of how priorities and strategies can be structured and addressed in a collections plan. In addition, other noted problem areas included developing the vision for the collection, breaking through administrative resistance or lack of commitment, and assessing the strengths and weaknesses of existing collections. Figure 5.1 illustrates the barriers identified as the biggest challenges to collections planning. The survey yielded valuable data, which, coupled with research, has been used to develop a list of helpful hints to facilitate collections planning in small museums. Respondents had learned about collections planning through museum literature, academic degree programs, conferences, assessments, and other training opportunities.

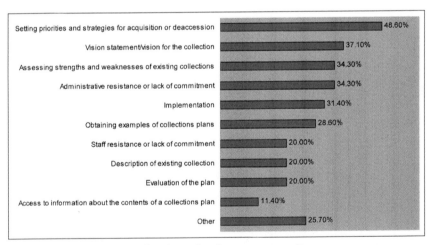

Figure 5.1. Barriers to collections planning survey results.

Helpful Hints for Collections Planning in Small Museums

1. Focus first on why your institution needs a collections plan. If you cannot convince yourself about the need for collections planning, you will not succeed in convincing others.

2. Engaging in top-down or bottom-up planning (much less hiring a consultant) may not be an option for small museums without full-time staff. In many smaller museums, board members play a more active role in day-to-day activities. Consider appointing one or two board members to serve on the collections planning committee.

3. Seek assistance and support from peer institutions in your region. Consider forming an alliance or collections planning support group to pool professional knowledge about and resources on collections planning. As a group, you might be able to petition your state historic preservation office or museum affiliate group to sponsor a workshop on collections planning to educate staff, administrators, and board members about the importance of collections planning. The workshop could serve as a springboard to commitment from your leadership and staff buy-in.

4. Do not assume that getting staff buy-in will be easy. Start by getting leadership commitment and support from your director and board. Getting the buy-in of staff is the key to completing your collections plan, but be ready for resistance. Be prepared to adjust your approach for staff or volunteers who are resistant to collections planning.

5. Form a committee and start by listing all the pertinent components that you think should be in your institution's plan. Appoint someone to record minutes.

6. Be aware that the number of staff people involved and the depth of their involvement in your institution could affect how long the plan takes to complete.

7. Obtain copies of collections plans from similar institutions. Once you finish your plan, consider offering it to the AAM Information Center to be used as an example for other institutions.

8. Do not be afraid to delegate. The document should not be written exclusively by one person, but someone will need to take responsibility for giving it a common voice and making it cohesive. Create specific assignments for other staff or board members and set deadlines for completion.

9. Be prepared for the process to take a long time. As with many outcomes in museums, taking incremental steps is the only reasonable way to accomplish goals. Small museums usually have limited staff and resources, so consider devising a plan to write the plan. What can you reasonably expect to accomplish in six months amid current high-priority projects? Complete the plan in small, manageable bursts.

10. No rule states that a collections plan must be drafted in a linear fashion, starting with a preamble and ending with a schedule for review of the plan. Many institutions combine sections or simply omit those that are not relevant or viable at a particular time. For example, it is pretty common to see the historical overview of collections in the first part of the plan along with the purpose of the document and mission of the institution. In short, different institutions will organize their collections plans differently.

11. Focus on accuracy, not length, as you are drafting the collections plan. Plans can be too short or too long, but focus first simply on getting ideas down on paper. Likewise, know when to just set the plan aside. If you are having difficulty with a particular section, move on to another part, or do something else for a brief period.

12. Lack of an inventory will hinder the collections planning process. It is impossible to know what collections you need if you do not know what you already have. If collection data is fully entered into a computerized collections management system, it will be much easier to access complete and accurate information. A digital database is not essential to start the process but will certainly make the task of analyzing the existing collections much easier.

13. Include definitions of commonly used terms in your collections plan.

14. Be prepared to circulate multiple drafts of the plan. It is vital that all stakeholders have an opportunity to comment on it. Consider formulating a small focus group of nonstaff community members to gather feedback and ensure the document is understandable to a diverse audience.

15. Be aware that collections planning may result in the creation of new projects. As collections are analyzed, you will no doubt identify additional projects requiring attention. Projects have a way of multiplying, but try to stay focused on the task at hand. Record what needs to be done for projects in the future.

16. Use the plan by thinking outside the box. The utility of your freshly minted collections plan extends beyond enabling you to make strategic decisions about your collections. The vision for the collections

can be a valuable fundraising tool because you have a unified direction and sense of purpose. Portions of the collections plan, or the plan itself, will be useful in grant applications. If you are fortunate enough to be able to hire additional staff, the collections plan can also be used to help determine whether new staff members are a good fit for your institution.

17. Consider applying for funds to complete a full inventory or to support collections planning activities through the Institute of Museum and Library Services' Museums for America grant program.[13] In addition, the National Endowment for the Humanities' (NEH) Preservation Assistance Grants for Smaller Institutions[14] can be used for general preservation assessments. Assessments report on the condition of collections and make recommendations for future preservation activities. Small and midsize institutions that have never received an NEH grant are especially encouraged to apply to this program.

Collections stewardship is a fundamental responsibility of all collecting institutions and individuals charged with collections care, management, and accessibility. This chapter has stressed the importance of collections stewardship, the difference between collections policy and planning, and the relevance and significance of collections planning for institutions. We hope readers have gained the knowledge and confidence necessary to initiate a conversation about collections planning at their institutions. Raising awareness of the meaning and importance of collections planning is a vital first step. Many institutions may not be ready to begin the process of collections planning, but this chapter argues at least that collections planning should become a short- or long-term institutional goal. Collections planning builds institutional capacity. This capacity manifests itself in critical thinking about the scope, purpose, and future of our collections and collecting goals to ensure that what we do with our collections has value to our mission and the communities we serve.

Bibliography and Resource List

American Association of Museums (AAM). "American Association of Museums: Characteristics of Excellence for U.S. Museums." AAM. www.aam-us.org/museum resources/map/upload/Characteristics-page-FNL.pdf (accessed June 29, 2010).

———. "Collections Planning." AAM. www.aam-us.org/museumresources/ic/cs/cp/index.cfm (accessed June 29, 2010).

Buck, Rebecca A., and Jean Allman Gilmore. *Collection Conundrums: Solving Collections Management Mysteries*. Washington, DC: American Association of Museums, 2007.

———, eds. *Museum Registration Methods*. 5th ed. Washington, DC: American Association of Museums Press, 2010.

Cato, Paisley S., Julia Golden, and Suzanne B. McLaren, eds. *Museum Wise: Workplace Words Defined*. Washington, DC: Society for the Preservation of Natural History Collections, 2003.

Collections Australia Network. "Significance—a Guide to Assessing the Significance of Cultural Heritage Objects and Collections." Collections Australia. www.collections australia.net/sector_info_item/5 (accessed June 29, 2010).

Gardner, James B., and Elizabeth E. Merritt. *The AAM Guide to Collections Planning*. Washington, DC: American Association of Museums, 2004.

———. "Collections Planning: Pinning Down a Strategy." *Museum News* (July–August 2002): 30–33, 60–61.

Lord, Gail Dexter. *Forward Planning and the Cost of Collecting*. New York: Lord Cultural Resources Planning and Management Inc., 1989.

Lucas, Frederick A. "The Evolution of the Museum." *Proceedings of the American Association of Museums Meeting* (June 4–6, 1907): 82–91.

Malaro, Marie C. *A Legal Primer on Managing Museum Collections*. 2nd ed. Washington, DC: Smithsonian Institution Press, 1998.

———. "Legal and Ethical Foundations of Museum Collecting Policies." In *Libraries, Museums, and Archives: Legal Issues and Ethical Challenges in the New Information Era*, edited by Tomas A. Lipinski, 69–82. Lanham, MD: Scarecrow, 2002.

Merritt, Elizabeth E., *National Standards and Best Practices for U.S. Museums*. Washington, DC: American Association of Museums, 2008.

Oehlschlaeger-Garvey, Barb. "How to . . . Develop a Collections Plan." *Illinois Association of Museums* 38 (2005): 1–4.

Reibel, Daniel B. *Registration Methods for the Small Museum*. 4th ed. Walnut Creek, CA: AltaMira Press, 2008.

Schwarzer, Marjorie. *Riches, Rivals, and Radicals: 100 Years of Museums in America*. Washington, DC: American Association of Museums, 2006.

Simmons, John E. "Managing Things: Crafting a Collections Management Policy." *Museum News* (January–February 2004): 29–31, 47–48.

———. *Things Great and Small: Collections Management Policies*. Washington, DC: American Association of Museums, 2006.

Sullivan, Martin. "Introduction: Collections Stewardship and Collections Planning." In *The AAM Guide to Collections Planning*, edited by James B. Gardner and Elizabeth E. Merritt, 1–3. Washington, DC: American Association of Museums, 2004.

Vaughan, James. "Introduction: The Call for a National Conversation." *Forum Journal* (spring 2008): 5–9.

Notes

1. Most recently, Elizabeth Merritt stated that "a fifth of museums report that they do not own, care for or use collections," in "Museums: A Snapshot," *Museum News* (January–February 2010): 56.

2. Data obtained from "Frequently Asked Questions about Museums," American Association of Museums, www.aam-us.org/aboutmuseums/abc.cfm (accessed June 29, 2010).

3. Data taken from Heritage Preservation and the Institute of Museum and Library Services, *A Public Trust at Risk: The Heritage Health Index Report on the State of America's Collections*, Heritage Preservation, 2005, www.heritagepreservation.org/hhi (accessed June 29, 2010).

4. See Randi Korn, "The Case for Holistic Intentionality," *Curator* 50, no. 2 (April 2007), for a discussion of how the notion of intentionality can impact and reinforce a museum's mission.

5. This definition of a small museum was taken in part from the definition established by the American Association for State and Local History (AASLH) Small Museums Committee. The full definition is available at "Small Museums Committee and Affinity Group," AASLH, www.aaslh.org/SmallMuseums.htm (accessed June 29, 2010).

6. Quoted from "American Association of Museums: Characteristics of Excellence for U.S. Museums in Plain English," American Association of Museums, www.aam-us.org/museumresources/map/upload/Characteristics-page-FNL.pdf (accessed June 29, 2010).

7. For more information, please see "StEPs: Standards and Excellence Program for History Organizations," AASLH, www.aaslh.org/steps.htm (accessed June 29, 2010).

8. This percentage was calculated based on the 779 accredited museums out of approximately 17,500 museums as of January 2010 ("Accreditation Program Annual Statistics At-a-Glace," AAM, www.aam-us.org/museumresources/accred/upload/2010-Accred-Annual-Stats-At-A-Glance.pdf [accessed June 29, 2010]).

9. The authors identified two collections plans available online as of January 2010. These include, but are not limited to, "Pratt Museum Collections Plan," Pratt Museum: Art, Science & Culture of Kachemak Bay, Alaska, www.prattmuseum.org/collections/linked_pages/collectionsplan.html, and "Collection Plan," Witte Museum, San Antonio, Texas, http://collections.wittemuseum.org/pdfs/Collection%20Plan%20Final%20 11-28-2007%20%282%29.pdf (accessed June 29, 2010).

10. See the bibliography and resource list for a link to the AAM fact sheets online.

11. Definitions of commonly used museum terminology can be found in Cato et al. (2003) and Merritt (2008).

12. The survey consisted of ten questions; it was designed and data was collected using SurveyMonkey. The survey was circulated over the RC-AAM, AASLH Small Museums, and AAMG (formerly ACUMG) e-mail distribution lists.

13. The Collections Stewardship (Management of Collections) category supports activities—including inventory and collections planning—that museums undertake to maintain and improve the management of museum collections in order to fulfill the museum's public service mission. See "Grant Applicants: Available Grants: Museums for America," IMLS, www.imls.gov/applicants/grants/forAmerica.shtm (accessed June 29, 2010).

14. See "Preservation Assistance Grants for Smaller Institutions," NEH, www.neh .gov/grants/guidelines/pag.html (accessed June 29, 2010).

CONSERVATION PLANNING

Julie A. Reilly

H ow does the staff at a small museum begin the process of conservation for its collection? What does the volunteer, curator, or administrator at a small museum, historical society, or historic house museum mean by conservation of the collection? What does the board member responsible for the oversight of the small museum mean by conservation? What does a conservator mean by conservation? Are the answers to these questions different for small museums? In small museums, conservators are rarely involved in everyday decisions about the care of the collection, the allocation of scarce resources, or the establishment of priorities within the museum. The absence of conservators in the small museum workplace is partly due to the small number of practicing conservators, the fact that most conservators work in larger institutions, and the lower level of financial resources generally available to smaller institutions for conservation services. The infrequency of communication with conservators about caring for collections in small institutions has resulted in an often awkward situation where the museum staff know they should be working with a conservator but cannot afford to pay one. The staff may also suspect that even if the museum could afford conservation consulting fees, the conservator's recommendations would not be financially feasible for the institution. However, when conservators and small museum volunteers and staff do find a way to work together on projects such as collections care, preventive conservation, or fundraising, the experience is extremely rewarding, and the end result is significantly better than when either works alone.

> The care and responsible conservation of collections can only be successfully achieved when both small museum staff and conservators work together.

Conservation

Conservation describes the activities that preserve and protect cultural resources. It includes object examination, documentation, treatment, stabilization, restoration, and preventive care. Conservation seeks to minimize physical and chemical damage to collections through both preventive care practices and actual conservation treatments. Several fundamental tenets of conservation include the need to preserve the significance and contextual information of an object, the desire to prevent as much damage to an object as possible, and the desire to interfere with the material state of the object as little as possible.

Preventive Conservation

Preventive conservation (used interchangeably with preventive care) seeks to protect collections from deterioration and damage through the formulation and implementation of policies and procedures that deal with environmental conditions, object handling, storage, exhibition, use (including consumptive use), integrated pest management, packing, transport, emergency preparedness, reproduction, reformatting, and duplication. The goal of preventive conservation is to diminish the daily stresses on collections, which build up over time, and to avoid catastrophic damage or loss.

Conservation Treatment

Conservation treatment is the intentional intervention in or alteration of the physical or chemical state of an object with the intent to prolong its lifespan. Treatment may be as simple as stabilization, which preserves the current status or condition of an object and minimizes further deterioration. Interventive treatment can be performed to return an object to a previous state of better preservation structurally, materially, or, sometimes, cosmetically. Cosmetic treatment is usually referred to as restoration and generally involves the addition of new materials. Conservation treatments are thoroughly documented in written reports with accompanying images and sketches. When preventive conservation is effective, interventive conservation treatment and restoration are rarely needed.

> Preventive conservation is the most efficient and cost-effective means of protecting cultural heritage.

> When preventive care practices are effective, conservation treatments will also rarely be necessary.

Conservators

A conservator is a professional who, through training, knowledge, and professional experience, engages in the work of conservation. This practitioner is skilled in both the theories and practices of preventive conservation and interventive conservation treatment. Generally, a conservator will specialize in specific types of materials (e.g., books, photographic materials, paintings, decorative arts, textiles). The role of the conservator is to assess the condition of objects; perform conservation treatments; complete condition surveys; identify signs and causes of deterioration; provide information and advice about the environment and object handling; recommend preventive care practices; and conduct research.

The American Institute for Conservation (AIC) is a national membership organization for conservators that advances and promotes the importance of the preservation of cultural property.[1] Professional associate and fellow members agree to practice conservation in accordance with the "Code of Ethics and Guidelines for Practice" established by the membership, copies of which are available to read or download on the AIC website.[2] This organization has categories of membership based on interest, qualification, and fitness to further the purposes of the AIC. The AIC maintains a list of professional associate and fellow member conservators by geographic region, area of specialization, and category of membership, which can be used to search for and find conservators for specific projects.[3]

Determining the Need for Conservation

A small museum should fully understand its purpose as a collections-holding institution and its collections policies before undertaking any conservation work. What is the significance of your collection? Is your collection important for its aesthetic qualities? Is it a research collection? Is the collection unique? Does it have historic significance? Individual objects in a collection may be important for one or all these reasons. The place of an artifact in a collection will determine its conservation needs. Archival collections with objects that are important for their

> The nature of the collection is an important determinant in the degree and type of conservation it will need. Know why your collection should be conserved.

historic and cultural content often do not receive extensive cosmetic conservation procedures; instead, efforts are directed toward preserving the content and not necessarily the appearance of the original materials. Objects in research collections are conserved with the intent to prevent interference with their research potential. Art collections often receive more attention to cosmetic or aesthetic problems. Ethnographic and folk art collections are often stabilized but not restored to a previous or new appearance.

The size and scope of a collection also determines its conservation needs. Only when familiar with the depth and breadth of a collection can a museum prioritize its care. So an important step in laying the foundation for collections conservation is to prepare a complete collections inventory and, if possible, an accompanying catalog with photo documentation. Why is this so important? If a conservator is asked to prepare condition assessments for a group of similar objects (say, marbles), and the marbles have not been inventoried and assigned valid object numbers, how can the conservator convey that one marble needs attention and another does not? Who will know which condition assessment and recommendation goes with which marble? How can the information generated about a group of thirty marbles be associated to each specific marble if the objects are not numbered and the numbers are not associated with the objects? Generally, for this reason, conservators will not assess or survey collections that are not cataloged and inventoried. Knowing why a collection is important, what is in it, and how many of each item is present helps the curator and conservator determine how much work may be needed and what parts of the collection may be of higher priority than other parts.

> Know what objects you have and how many objects you have.

> Have a collections management plan or policy in place.

Additionally, an institution should have a sound collections management policy or collections plan in place that describes and supports preventive conservation activities. This document sets down in writing the institution's professional standards and practices, which should follow standards set by the American Association of Museums and American Association for State and Local History.

Conservation Planning

The Conservation Assessment

The first step in the conservation process is to complete a conservation assessment, a tool designed to help smaller institutions learn about their current ability to care for their collections and meet current standards for professional collections care practice. A conservation assessment offers prioritized recommendations for both short- and long-term collections care activities and forms the baseline for the development of a long-term conservation plan. The assessment results in a detailed written report on the policies, practices, and conditions within an institution that impact collection survival. The goal of a conservation assessment is to assist and inform the on-site staff, board, and volunteers and to recommend priority actions to improve collections care and conservation for the collection.[4] (See chapter 1 in Book 1 for more information about assessment programs.)

Getting a Conservation Assessment

Conservation assessments are performed by experienced assessors and can be arranged through a technical assistance program of the Institute of Museum and Library Services (IMLS) called the Conservation Assessment Program (CAP). Heritage Preservation manages the CAP program. The awards are

> The first step in the conservation process is to have a conservator complete a conservation assessment.

noncompetitive in that they are first come, first served. There is no required match for the program awards, but a minimal amount of financial contribution is required by the institution to cover all the assessment costs. To find out more about the CAP program, call Heritage Preservation or visit its website.[5]

Conservation assessments are also often completed outside of the CAP program. A conservator or architectural assessor can be engaged directly by your institution. Funding can come from operational sources, donations, or other grant programs, such as the IMLS's Conservation Project Support (CPS) grants.[6] CAP grants through Heritage Preservation are designated for smaller institutions, but CPS grants can be awarded for assessments of larger institutions. Assessments usually cost around $4,000 per assessor plus travel and other expenses.

Choosing Your Assessor or Conservator

The best way to find a conservator is through personal references from your colleagues. If you are in an area with fewer conservators, you can find the nearest one using the referral list on the AIC website.[7] This website's "How to Choose a Conservator" page can be read online.[8] If you receive your assessment through the CAP program, Heritage Preservation will send a list of approved and experienced assessors with the announcement of your CAP award. However you find conservators for the work you would like to have done, you should ask for a resume and a list of references. The conservator should be able to send samples of any work he or she has completed that is comparable to the project you have in mind. You should talk with the conservator over the phone or in person to ensure a good fit between you, your institution, and the conservator. As in other areas, it cannot hurt to get a second opinion about a problem or another estimate for a project.

The conservator you choose to help with a conservation assessment can become a long-term ally and consultant for your museum. This person will have a great overall knowledge of your institution and collection after the assessment process and can help suggest helpful resources like publications and websites. He or she can provide quick consultations and would be the perfect candidate to help not only with conservation planning but also with emergency, pest management, storage, and strategic planning for your museum. The conservator would be the perfect contact in the event of an emergency.

A Long-Range Conservation Plan

The completed conservation assessment report should be used to develop a long-range conservation plan. Stakeholders from your institution should be

> After the conservation assessment, prepare a long-range conservation plan.

drawn together to form a conservation planning group to blend institutional priorities and integrate the assessment recommendations. As with all long-range planning, efforts can be advanced on several fronts simultaneously, taking into account long-range and short-range improvements. The conservation or preservation plan should be in written form and should explain all assumptions about the collection, any rationales used, and the museum's goals. The items in the long-range plan may include preventive conservation, conservation assessment, and treatment measures. Preventive measures might include intellectual control improvements (completing an inventory, finishing the cataloguing, adding photo documentation) and physical control improvements (improving environmental conditions and storage, monitoring the environment, upgrading exhibition methods). The conservation assessment report and the long-range plan should detail the preventive measures that should be taken to preserve the collection.

The conservation planning process should also clearly indicate which parts of the collection are most significant to the institution and which parts are likely to be in the most need of conservation. The planning process will determine which parts of the collection should be the first to receive a deeper level of conservation evaluation through a conservation condition survey.

The Conservation Condition Survey: Object by Object

A conservation condition survey examines individual objects in a collection for their specific conservation needs. The process involves examining each object in the collection or portion of the collection and recording object condition, treatment needs, housing needs, exhibition recommendations, and storage needs. For example, a paper conservator can evaluate all or part of the paper artifacts in your collection. An objects conservator can survey the objects in your collection. In general, a conservation condition survey covers a discrete portion of a collection, although in some cases complete collection condition surveys are undertaken.

Prior to the survey visit, the conservator should prepare a survey form in consultation with the museum staff, taking into account the specifics of the collection and the museum. The form will determine what data will be collected as part of the survey. The data collected should make it possible to answer the

> With the long-range conservation plan in place and recommended preventive measures under way, consider having conservators complete collection condition surveys.

questions prompting the survey. Each item is individually examined unless the collection is prohibitively large, as is the case with archival or archaeological collections, in which case, random sampling is used to select items for individual examination, or groups of similar objects can be examined together as a group and reported en masse on the same survey sheet.

Survey data should include identifying information about each object—accession number, catalog number, date accessioned, location, size, shape, primary and secondary materials, techniques of manufacture, artist or maker, country of origin, and so forth. This data can often be downloaded from existing collection databases. The survey should provide a conservation priority for each item examined that takes into account the condition of the object, its treatment needs, the relative urgency of the object's condition in comparison to that of other objects in the survey, and the skill level of the practitioner needed to do the recommended work. This system will allow the objects in the survey to be ranked numerically by their overall conservation priority. The survey should record clearly defined information about the condition of each object as well. Condition rankings should be explicit and agreed upon before the survey begins. (See textbox 6.1 for an example.)

The next ranking needed to establish an object's conservation priority is its treatment need or priority. Treatment priority measures the level of intervention the object requires and its urgency (see textbox 6.2 for an example). The treatment ranking should be integrated with a measure of the object's curatorial or

---

TEXTBOX 6.1

SAMPLE CONDITION RANKINGS FOR SURVEYS

5 Excellent condition, no problems
4 Very good condition, minimal superficial problems
3 Good condition, minor structural and/or superficial problems
2 Fair condition, moderate structural problems and/or surface deterioration
1 Poor condition, major structural and/or surface deterioration

---

TEXTBOX 6.2

SAMPLE TREATMENT PRIORITY RANKINGS FOR SURVEYS

6   Needs no treatment
5   Needs preventive measures
4   Needs cleaning or very minor intervention
3   Needs minor treatment when possible
2   Needs major treatment as soon as possible
1   Needs immediate or major conservation attention

---

institutional significance to the collection and the museum as well. The institutional priority must be determined by the curator and museum staff and can also be expressed in a ranking system (see textbox 6.3 for an example). For example, objects actually owned by a founder or principle historic figure associated with the museum would be of higher institutional priority than replacement period antiques, which would be of higher priority than modern reproduction items produced to fill a void in the collection.

The survey data should also include listings of the specific work that should be done to preserve each object. A survey form can indicate the need for simple dusting or covering in storage to upgrades in exhibit display methods to actual interventive treatments, such as rust mitigation for iron objects (see textbox 6.4 for other examples).

If the survey information is detailed enough, these listings can be very helpful in discussing and arranging for future treatment cost estimates. The

---

TEXTBOX 6.3

SAMPLE INSTITUTIONAL PRIORITY RANKINGS FOR SURVEYS

4   The object is not significant to the collection
3   The object is a study/demonstration object
2   The object is a valued part of the collection
1   The object is an essential part of the collection
0   Not applicable

TEXTBOX 6.4

SAMPLE WORK RECOMMENDATIONS FOR SURVEYS

- Reapply coating
- Consolidate flaking surface
- Fill losses
- Apply protective coating
- Special housing required
- Special mount required
- Micro-environment recommended
- Minimize handling

surveyor should indicate the amount of time the suggested work would take to complete, and from the time estimates, cost estimates can be calculated. Another very helpful distinction to include in the survey process is an indication of the type of practitioner needed to perform the preservation or conservation actions being recommended (see textbox 6.5 for an example). For example, on-site staff can usually complete many preventive improvements to storage conditions, particularly if there is an opportunity for the conservator to train the staff in advance.

If the survey information is thought through carefully in advance with the conservator and the museum's staff, it can become a powerful planning tool in understanding the needs of the collection and in quantifying and qualifying the

TEXTBOX 6.5

SAMPLE PRACTITIONER-TYPE CODING FOR SURVEYS

5 No work is needed
4 After training, site staff can complete the work
3 Under close supervision by a conservator, a technician can complete the work
2 A conservator is needed to complete the work
1 A specialist conservator is needed to complete the work

number, type, and scope of projects that should be undertaken to preserve and, if needed, conserve the collection. On average, roughly only 10 to 15 percent of the typical collection will require interventive conservation treatment by a conservator for preservation. A large majority of objects usually require only preventive measures for long-term survival. On-site staff and volunteers can often perform many of the recommended preventive procedures after training and with the guidance of a conservator. Although curatorial professionals are often taught to do condition reporting themselves, they are rarely able to associate condition issues with specific sources of deterioration or with relevant recommendations for treatment or preventive care measures. Curatorial assistance in documenting the condition of objects during a survey might be feasible; a conservator should make all the ranking decisions and select all the recommendations for the survey. Using database software for the survey makes it possible to use the variety of information generated to define projects that will move collections care and conservation forward. Survey data can be set up so that the information can be mathematically manipulated. An overall conservation priority score can be calculated for each object as shown in textbox 6.6.

The lower the score, the higher and more urgent the preservation needs for the object. The entire collection could conceivably be ranked in order using this system. The survey data will indicate which items, at what priority, require what kind of conservation work by what kind of practitioner, which will take how much time and require how much money. A well-designed collection survey can be an extremely powerful planning tool and an indispensable adjunct to the long-range conservation plan.

Conservation Treatment

After a conservation assessment, preservation planning, and a collection survey, it is finally time to consider individual object treatments. Ironically, many museum staff, volunteers, and board members think conservation treatment of individual objects is conservation of the collection, when in reality this comes at the end of the long conservation planning process!

TEXTBOX 6.6

Overall conservation priority score = object condition ranking + treatment priority ranking + practitioner-type code + institutional priority ranking.

> After you complete collection condition surveys, high-priority objects should be selected for conservation treatment.

The conservation treatment process for an individual object must begin with an examination report and a treatment proposal. The examination report should describe the object and its materials, manufacture, maker or artist, appearance, and condition. The treatment proposal should systematically recommend treatment procedures to correct condition problems and to preserve and conserve the object. Current conservation professional practice standards require an examination report and treatment proposal prior to the start of any work on the object. The treatment proposal must be signed and approved by a museum representative before any work is undertaken. The proposal should also come with a clear, not-to-exceed estimate of the costs for the work. After the conservation treatment is completed, the conservator should send the museum a treatment report detailing the work done, including the materials and techniques used, with all photo documentation recorded.[9] As discussed above, conservation treatments range in the level of intervention required and should seek to intervene as little as needed to address the condition issues.

TEXTBOX 6.7

CONSERVATION PLANNING SUMMARY

1. Know why your collection is important.
2. Know what objects you have and how many objects you have.
3. Have a collections management plan or policy in place.
4. Complete a conservation assessment with a conservator.
5. Write a long-range conservation plan with your stakeholders.
6. Implement the plan through preventive measures.
7. Implement the plan through conservation collection surveys (object by object).
8. Implement the plan through conservation treatment of individual objects.
9. Update the long-range conservation plan as you achieve its goals or as the collection or institution changes.

Case History: The Abbe Museum[10]

The Abbe Museum of Bar Harbor, Maine, offers innovative exhibitions and programs on Maine's Native American heritage. In recent years, the Abbe has grown from a small trailside museum privately operated within Acadia National Park into an exciting contemporary museum in the heart of downtown Bar Harbor.

The museum has seriously and responsibly approached the conservation and preservation of its collection for over twenty-five years. Beginning as early as 1986, the Abbe has engaged professional conservators to assess the care of the collection and to examine the condition of objects. The consulting conservators have made recommendations to improve collections care and preservation, and the museum has persistently and successfully implemented the changes recommended to the significant betterment of its collection.

The conservation planning process began in 1986 when a conservator working with the statewide museum services program in Maine recommended that the Abbe undertake a conservation assessment. This initial assessment resulted in recommendations for structural changes and passive measures to improve environmental control for the museum. Projects undertaken included improvements to the building envelope: drainage, sealing, weatherproofing, insulation, gutter and downspout maintenance, environmental monitoring, and ultraviolet light protection. The assessor also recommended initial steps to clean and re-house the collections in storage and to invest in the training of museum staff in preventive care methods and practices.

In 1991, the Institute of Museum Services supported long-range conservation planning for the Abbe relating to a future building project. The recommendations that resulted from this planning, recorded in a 1994 long-range conservation plan, included continued environmental control and monitoring activities, the preparation of an emergency preparedness plan, continued building repairs, and the first collection condition survey for a portion of the collection, which led to the first conservation treatments of collection objects.

This long-range conservation plan was evaluated and augmented in 1998 and 1999, when a second conservation assessment was completed. Recommendations and goals featured rodent control; improved storage furniture, methods, and materials; upgrades to pest control and the emergency plan; and continued planning for a new museum building with proper collection storage facilities.

In 2002, a new building was completed, and transfer of collections to the new storage locations was initiated. In 2003, the long-range conservation plan was updated again to include both the new and old facilities. Recommendations addressed heating, ventilating, and air conditioning (HVAC) issues and monitoring for the new facility, emergency plan updates, more collection condition surveys, more individual object treatments, and more staff training. The plan was updated again in 2003, 2005, 2006, and 2009. The museum completed its third conservation assessment in 2011.

The Abbe Museum clearly has a long and very successful track record of cyclical assessment, evaluation, planning, and implementation of measures to ensure the long-term preservation of its collections. Some issues have been resolved. Some ongoing issues, like emergency planning, integrated pest management, and environmental control procedures, have become integrated into institutional policy and practice. Others issues, like HVAC performance and equipment upgrades, have proven to be ongoing problems but continue to be addressed and discussed as goals in the Abbe's long-range conservation plan.

> The overall results of our museum's conservation program have been positive— and all . . . without the input of large amounts of capital. . . . Now we *know* that we are taking good care of our collections. Although there is no conservator on staff, we recognize the problems and feel confident.[11]
>
> —Dianne R. Kopec, director, Abbe Museum, 1991

Conclusions

This chapter has discussed the basic course for the responsible conservation of collections. Clearly, one must have the advice and input of consultants in different specializations to make this stepped effort a success. Financial resources are required and can come from many sources, such as grant awards, donations, and operational funds (established through dedicated budgetary line items). Staff, volunteers, and board members must be available to assist with the assessment, conduct the strategic long-range planning, and implement preservation and conservation recommendations.

The path to collections conservation may seem overwhelming, so it is best to take conservation or collections care steps in the proper sequence—from assessment and conservation planning to individual object treatment. The sequence of assessment and planning steps set forth above (and reviewed in textbox 6.7) constitutes the best path toward the responsible conservation of your collections. Assessment and planning will help ensure that scarce resources are most efficiently and effectively allocated for the activities that will best preserve the collections for the future. With limited money, staff, volunteers, and training opportunities, the conservation of a collection can seem an impossible goal to many small museums. Each achievement, however small, should be celebrated and shared. Each realistic goal set and achieved is a step in the right direction.

Notes

1. See the American Institute for Conservation website at www.conservation-us.org.

2. "Code of Ethics and Guidelines for Practice," American Institute for Conservation, www.conservation-us.org/index.cfm?fuseaction=page.viewPage&pageID=858&nodeID=1.

3. "Resource Center: Find a Conservator," American Institute for Conservation, www.conservation-us.org/index.cfm?fuseaction=Page.viewPage&pageId=495.

4. Sara Wolf, ed., *The Conservation Assessment: A Tool for Planning, Implementing, and Fund-Raising* (Washington, DC: Getty Conservation Institute and Heritage Preservation, 1991), 2.

5. Contact Heritage Preservation at (202) 233-0800 or www.heritagepreservation.org.

6. See the Institute of Museum and Library Services website at www.imls.gov.

7. American Institute for Conservation, "Resource Center: Find a Conservator."

8. "Resource Center: How to Choose a Conservator," American Institute for Conservation, www.conservation-us.org/index.cfm?fuseaction=Page.viewPage&pageId=1345.

9. American Institute for Conservation, "Code of Ethics and Guidelines for Practice."

10. See the Abbe Museum website at www.abbemuseum.org.

11. Diane R. Kopec, "Conservation Cure," *Museum News* (May–June 1991): 60–63.

INDEX

of, 27–28; institutional mind-set, 31; irreversible damage from, 26; managing, 29; preventing damage from, 29; preventive conservation checklist, 29–30; written policy, 29–30; written procedure, 30

HVAC. *See* heating, ventilating, and air conditioning

ICS. *See* Incident Command System

identification, 70–72

identity, 44

Image Permanence Institutes Preservation Calculator, 37

image use: collections management policy and, 102–3; fees, 103

IMLS. *See* Institute of Museum and Library Services

Incident Command System (ICS), 33, 37–38; course in, 35; scaling, 38

Institute of Museum and Library Services (IMLS), 129, 136, 144

insulation, 50

integrated pest management (IPM), 16, 44; main areas of, 17

intellectual control, 63; maintaining, 65–66, 121

Internal Revenue Service Form 8283, 70

Internet, 67

inventory, 79–80

IPM. *See* integrated pest management

Johnston, Tamara, 76–77

KE EMu, 68

key policy, 29, 31

Klingler, Stacy, xii

Kopec, Dianne R., 145

landscaping, 48–49; action plan, 52–54; consultants, 53; mission and, 53; resources, 60; sustainability and, 53. *See also* cultural landscape report

lead, 21

A Legal Primer on Managing Museum Collections (Malaro), 1, 69

light: acceptable range of, 11; balanced approach to, 12; collections care and, 8–14; comfortable, 12; compact fluorescent, 14; damage from, 8–9; defining, 8; education, 12; effects of, *10*; energy-efficient, 14; eye adapting to, 11; frequently asked questions, 13–14; in historic house museums, 14; institutional mind-set, 13; measuring, 10–11, 12; meters, 10; preventive conservation checklist, 13; sixty days' exposure to, *9*; ultraviolet (UV), 8, 12, 13; visible, 8

loans, 81–82; American Precision Museum and, 99; collections management policy, 97–98; forms, 81; guidelines, 81; incoming, 98, 99; long-term, 81, 98; outgoing, 99

local emergency responders, 35, 38

loyalty, duty of, 111

Lucas, Frederick A., 108

lux, 10–11

Magnolia Grove and Gaineswood, 49

Malaro, Marie, 1, 69

MAP. *See* Museum Assessment Program

marking: barrier coat, 75; documentation, 75–78; photographs, 77; standard, 75; unacceptable, 76–77

mat burn, 23

Meador-Woodruff, Robin, 76–77

Merritt, Elizabeth, 114, 117–19

metal-edged tags, 77

metric system, 11

Microsoft Access, 67

Milne, A. A., 26

mission, 45; collections management and, 63; collections management plan and, 121; intentionality and, 131n4; landscaping and, 53; review, 121; revising, 45; signage and, 54; supporting, 45

ABOUT THE EDITORS

Cinnamon Catlin-Legutko has worked in the small museum world since 1994 and was the director of the General Lew Wallace Study & Museum in Crawfordsville, Indiana, from 2003 to 2009. In 2008, the museum was awarded the National Medal for Museum Service. Her contributions to the field include leadership of the AASLH Small Museums Committee, service as an IMLS grant reviewer and AAM MAP peer reviewer, and service as an AASLH Council member. She is now CEO of the Abbe Museum in Bar Harbor, Maine.

Stacy Klingler currently serves local history organizations as the assistant director of local history services at the Indiana Historical Society. She began her career in museums as the assistant director of two small museums, before becoming director of the Putnam County Museum in Greencastle, Indiana. She chairs the AASLH's Small Museums Committee (2008–2012) and attended the Seminar for Historical Administration in 2006. While she lives in the history field, her passion is encouraging a love of learning in any environment.

ABOUT THE CONTRIBUTORS

Scott Carrlee has been working for the Alaska State Museums since August 2000. In 2006, after twenty years in conservation, he took the position as curator of museum services, supporting museum development and providing technical assistance to museums around Alaska. Through this position, he promotes the idea that the greatest tool yet invented for the preservation of objects is the museum itself.

Bruce Teeple is a freelance writer, local historian, speaker, gardener, chicken farmer, and columnist for the *Centre Daily Times* in State College, Pennsylvania. A graduate of Penn State in history and political science, he served for nineteen years as curator of the Aaronsburg Historical Museum before joining AASLH's Small Museums Committee. He is currently researching and writing *As Good As a Handshake: The Farringtons and the Political Culture of Moonshine in Central Pennsylvania.*

Patricia L. Miller is executive director of the Illinois Heritage Association, a nonprofit service organization based in Champaign, Illinois. She works with museums, libraries, and other cultural heritage organizations throughout the state. She is a peer reviewer for the American Association of Museums for the Accreditation and Museum Assessment programs. Miller is an adjunct lecturer in the history department at Eastern Illinois University, Charleston, where she has taught graduate classes in historic site administration since 1985.

Julia Clark is curator of collections at the Abbe Museum, Bar Harbor, Maine. She is responsible for all aspects of collections care and management and works with exhibits and facilities. She has a bachelor's degree in anthropology from Bowdoin College and a master's in anthropology from the University of Arkansas, with course work in museum studies. In her spare time, she is a captain in the Orland Fire Department and president of the Hancock County Firefighters Association.

Nicolette B. Meister is curator of collections of the Logan Museum of Anthropology and adjunct assistant professor of museum studies at Beloit College. She is on the board of *Collections: A Journal for Museum and Archives Professionals* and is a member of the American Association for State and Local History (AASLH) Small Museums Committee. She is also a program consultant and instructor for the Campbell Center for Historic Preservation Studies. She has a master's of science degree in museum and field studies from the University of Colorado, Boulder, and a bachelor's in anthropology from the University of Wisconsin, Milwaukee.

Jackie Hoff is currently the director of collections services at the Science Museum of Minnesota and is responsible for helping to inform the vision and participate in the design and implementation of programs that promote, develop, and sustain a focused and growing program of collection study and care, education, and research. She supervises the collections registration, conservation, database, and administrative functions. She also serves on the steering committee for the Minnesota Association of Museums.

Julie A. Reilly has served as a conservator, educator, administrator, and consultant for the Smithsonian Institution, the Colonial Williamsburg Foundation, Winterthur, the Winterthur/University of Delaware Art Conservation Program, the Nebraska State Historical Society (University of Nebraska, Lincoln), and the Ford Conservation Center. She holds a bachelor's degree from Towson State University and a master's from The George Washington University; she is an American Institute for Conservation fellow, an associate editor for the *Journal of the American Institute for Conservation*, and a National Peer Professional for the GSA Public Building Service's Design Excellence Program.